EXPRESSION IN MOVEMENT AND THE ARTS

LEPUS BOOKS
205 Gt.Portland St.London W1N 6LR

Expression in Movement & the Arts

A PHILOSOPHICAL ENQUIRY

David Best

David Best
M.A. (Cantab.), B.Phil. (York),
Leverhulme Fellow in the Department of Philosophy,
University College of Swansea;
formerly Senior Lecturer in Philosophy,
Chelsea College of Physical
Education.

© 1974 by Lepus Books

An associate company of Henry Kimpton Ltd.
205, Great Portland St., London W1N 6LR

SBN 0 86019 003 X

Computer Typesetting by Print Origination, Merseyside L20 6NS
Printed by T & A. Constable, Edinburgh EH 7 4NF

To

Magdalene College

Cambridge

CONTENTS

ACKNOWLEDGEMENTS

I am very grateful to the many colleagues and students at Chelsea College of Physical Education who have so generously and enthusiastically given their time to show me and talk about the interesting work they are doing in dance and other aspects of physical education. I should like to express my thanks to Hilary Corlett, Principal Lecturer in Art and Science of Movement, for discussing with me some of the issues here considered, and especially to Rita Arkley, the College Librarian, not only for her careful checking of the proofs, but also for her unstinted help in countless other ways. My thanks are due, too, to Bob Gleave for his care and expertise with the photographs, and to Sue Harding, whose fine quality of movement made such a splendid subject.

In am indebted to Renford Bambrough, Dean of St. John's College, Cambridge, whose seminal lectures and writings, especially with respect to the significance of the philosophy of Wittgenstein, set me thinking in directions which have helped me to clarify some of the problems of this enquiry.

My biggest debt is owed to Professor F.R. Atkinson, of the University of York, who was kind enough to read both the first and final drafts, whose detailed comments and advice have, throughout, been most helpful, and whose continued encouragement I greatly value.

INTRODUCTION

Philosophy is one subject. It is impossible, without serious danger of misconception, to conduct an isolated foray into one area of philosophy independently of philosophical thought in other areas. Insights achieved in one branch of enquiry may have significant repercussions in what may appear, at first sight, to be unrelated fields. Atkinson (1969) puts the point, in relation to moral philosophy, in this way:

> There are two points that I have throughout sought to emphasise above all others—one about morality, the other about moral philosophy. The former is that moral thinking is continuous with rational thinking generally; the latter that moral philosophy is continuous with the rest of philosophy.

It is still not often realised, outside philosophical circles, that there has been a revolution in philosophy in recent years, initiated by the later work of Wittgenstein. He did not have much to say directly on aesthetics or moral philosophy, but many of his suggestions with respect to other problems can be seen to have an important bearing on these two areas. This book is intended to introduce those whose concern is primarily with the arts to certain aspects of contemporary philosophical thought without which no consideration of aesthetics can be adequate. Writing and discussion of the arts is still too often characterised by what Elton (1954) calls "rapturous and soporific effusion". Work in this field is vitiated by underlying, misconceived presuppositions about, for example, meaning, reasoning and the emotions. I have tried to suggest ways in which changes of conception in such areas of enquiry relate to aesthetics, and where I have referred to Wittgenstein directly I have tried to explain what I think he meant by his remarks, since he is one of the most difficult philosophers to understand. Because of the importance of these references I have given paragraph or page numbers in his case.

The thesis here developed could, with appropriate adjustments, be applied to any of the arts. I have directed my attention mainly to dance for two reasons. First, despite the fact that it is a fine art form in its own right, dance has tended to be ignored, with one or two notable exceptions, by most writers on the philosophy of the arts. I hope to try to do a little to rectify that serious omission. And second, perhaps the most important of the philosophical areas of enquiry about which we need to be clear in order to understand *any* of the arts, is that of the relationship of mind to body—for example, what it means to speak of an emotion's being expressed in physical behaviour. In this respect dance is surely unique, for, though the issue concerns the other arts, there is an immediacy of the problem which is peculiar to the art of movement. The nearest to it is, perhaps, drama, but here there is the added complication of language. In dance the vehicle of aesthetic expression is physical movement, so the importance of being clear about the relation of the mind to the body, of how mental things can be expressed physically, is directly apparent.

It may strike some of those whose concerns are specifically with theories of dance that the argument which follows is somewhat remote and abstract. But we can become clear about meaning and expression in dance only if we first clarify the underlying philosophical confusions which have be-devilled discussion of the art of movement for so long. Frequently I discuss expression in actions generally, and have not specifically separated life emotions from aesthetic emotions. This is deliberate, since the problems involved are closely related. The philosophical problems involved in what it is for behaviour to express anger or fear are continuous with those concerning what is expressed in dance movement.

I do not wish to suggest that all art expresses emotions, or that what I have to say applies to all forms of dance. I think, however, that it would be fair to say that there is an intimate connection between much, if not most, art, and the emotions. My concern is with the expressiveness of some movements. And even where one may be doubtful about emotional content, "expression" is a natural word to use for the meaning of a work of art. Terminological differences would not affect the logical point which is my principal concern. Indeed, as I hope to show, disputes about termi-nology are sometimes the result of a failure adequately to diagnose some of the presuppositions which I am trying to expose.

Incidentally, though it is not my present concern, these same fallacious presuppositions, especially about the body/mind relationship, can be seen to vitiate much of what is said about other aspects of physical education. Examples which immediately occur to me are the tripartite division of the personality into thinking, feeling and doing aspects, with various claims made about integrating them, and theses about the development of the intellect and imagination through modern educational gymnastics.

For the most part I have used "aesthetic" and "artistic" interchangeably, though there are, of course, differences between them. For example, a sunset and an athletic movement, indeed almost, if not quite, anything can be considered from an aesthetic, though not from an artistic point of view. Nevertheless, this distinction is not, on the whole, important to my argument, and where it does become significant, I have drawn attention to it.

I have approached the problem of expression in movement through the notion of what the dancer is feeling. It may strike some readers that it is so obvious that the meaning of a dance is not, or at least is not always, what the performer feels that they may wonder why I adopt this line of argument.[1] I submit that there are, nevertheless, two advantages which accrue from approaching the problem in this way:

(a) Though admittedly incorrect as it stands, it is easier to grasp the logical character of the problem by means of this approach.

(b) This view does at least point in the right direction, as we shall see in section H(3), and there is a danger of overlooking this. Some writers on aesthetics recognise that a simple causal theory will not do, whether it identifies aesthetic meaning with the inner feeling which causes the external expression of the dancer, or with the inner feeling caused in the spectator by watching the dance. But they are led into more serious misconception by failing adequately to diagnose the underlying preconceptions of such a theory. Hence some of its most pernicious assumptions persist in the new theory, and even some valid aspects of the original view may be lost. Thus, for example, it may be said that dance expresses not what the dancer feels, but an abstract form of feeling. But to revise the theory in this way is to project the meaning of dance into a transcendental realm, and therefore to lose sight of the important truth in the former view, that aesthetic meaning is somehow inextricably bound up with human interests and emotions.

It is hoped that this book, though of interest to students

---

[1] In Fact it is far from being universally obvious. For instance. H'Doubler (1957) writes ". . . dance may be considered a neural projection of inner thought and feeling into movement," and ". . . art may be defined in its result as the adequate translation of emotional experience into some external form. It is the expression of the feeling within by means of line, or colour, or sound, or movement, so that others may share the feeling." And Hawkins (1964) seems to be thinking along the same lines in speaking of dance as "the expression of man's inner feelings". There are many such examples in the literature on dance.

of philosophy, will be comprehensible to the philosophically uninitiated, since it is to students, teachers and lecturers concerned with dance, the arts, and physical education that it is primarily directed. However, in my view, no philosophical problem can be made easy—one has to make any proposed solution one's own by thinking hard about it. Rush Rhees (1969):

> If you see the kind of difficulty that is raised in philosophy, you will see why there cannot be a simplified way of meeting it.
> This bears on the attitude which may be taken towards philosophy. I suppose someone might say: "I just want to play tennis; I don't care about playing it well." But for some reason you cannot say anything like this in philosophy. Unless you feel like taking philosophy *seriously,* then leave it alone.

So above all I should like to hope that this book might encourage those who read it to think more deeply about the philosophy of the arts in general, and about dance in particular. I am well aware that what I have written is, at best, only a pointer in a certain direction, and that much more work remains to be done, both in depth and in breadth, i.e. in further examination of the underlying rationale of the justification of aesthetic judgments, and in the application of the thesis here presented to particular problems in dance and the other arts. Though the former no doubt requires philosophical training, the latter can, perhaps, best be done by those whose expertise is in the field of dance or the teaching of dance and the arts generally, who want to examine more precisely what is said about their art.

In his preface Wittgenstein (1953) wrote:

> I should not like my writing to spare other people the trouble of thinking. But, if possible, to stimulate someone to thoughts of his own.

I cannot do better than echo that view.

We shall not cease from exploration
And the end of all our exploring
Will be to arrive where we started
And know the place for the first time.

T. S. Eliot. *Little Gidding*

A:

THE TRADITIONAL THEORY

What is expressed in movement?
What is expressed in art?
How is anything expressed in movement or in art?

At first sight it might appear that there is no great problem here, for such questions seem to be easily answered by statements which one frequently reads, hears, and indeed makes, such as:

"Movement expresses the inner qualities of a person."
"Movement of the human body has always been a medium for expressing the emotions."
"Movement expresses the personality."

One can readily call to mind many other remarks along these lines about the expressiveness of actions, and of art. Charlton (1970) says of the term "expression" that it seems the

"most appropriate word for the controlled and yet free and

creative activity of the artist: he does not describe or report his emotions, like a patient at the psychoanalyst, nor does he simply show them or let them be seen, like an ill-mannered person in company: he expresses them."

But what is meant by saying that actions and works of art express emotions? What is the connection between an intangible thing like an emotional state, and a physical thing like a human movement? The examples cited above typify the commonly held assumption that the action or work of art is an outward, observable manifestation of inner feelings or thoughts which, until they are revealed externally, are entirely private and known only to the person concerned. Thus the meaning of an expressive movement is given solely by the character of the emotion which it symbolises or stands for. One sometimes hears it said, for example, that dance springs from a love of expressive gesture. If we enquire what such gestures express, the usual answer is "emotions" or "feelings". And if we ask which emotions or feelings, a natural reply would be, "Those in the mind of the dancer, or choreographer".[1]

People often tend to talk in this way about works of art in every medium. Since the Romantic period theories of aesthetics have been predominantly expressionist, and are applied to the whole range of the arts. The word "expression" used in this context seems to remain closely related to its etymological derivation—*exprimere,* to squeeze out, as water may be squeezed out of a sponge. A point of some significance, as we shall see, is that the water which emerges is demonstrably the same as that which was contained in the sponge prior to the squeezing.

This, then, is the sort of analogy or metaphor which appears to underlie much of our unreflective psychological talk, not only in the context of aesthetics. The concept of mind which it presupposes is incorporated into our everyday

---

[1] I shall simply use "dancer" henceforth. Though there are, of course, differences between the performing and the non-performing arts, those differences are not relevant to the thesis of this book.

language. It presents a picture of a person experiencing a hidden, inner emotion which can emerge in various perceivable, material forms. Wordsworth, who is often regarded as the originator of Romantic expressionism, at least in English literature, captures this idea perfectly:

"All good poetry is the spontaneous overflow of powerful feelings."

Thus artistic expression is thought to be a release of feelings through the artist's particular medium, a sort of emotional catharsis. An emotion wells up inside and, to adapt Wordsworth, it spontaneously overflows into the physical movement of the dancer, or the manipulation of his paint and brush by the painter. The connection is usually supposed to be causal, in the sense that the inner emotion overflows and causes the external expressive action. Until it is revealed in this way, it is thought that only the person who experiences an emotion can know what he is feeling. So, to discover what is being expressed, other people observe the external action or work of art and infer from that to the inner emotional state which caused it. It is possible to do this because we all have inner feelings, and we know what it is like to express them outwardly. To take a simple case, if I see someone performing the outward action of sobbing, I can infer that her inner emotional state is one of extreme sadness. This inference is justified by my experience of the correlation between my own feeling of extreme sadness, and my tendency to behave in the same sort of way.

It is important to be quite clear about what is involved in making such an inference. As an illustration, consider the following hypothetical example. I have within sight of my study window an old windmill which is still in full working order. Whenever I glance out of the window and see the sails whirring round I am justified in inferring that there is a wind blowing. The inference is justified because I know from my own experience, and from what people tell me about their experience, that the wind, and only the wind, causes the sails to turn. There is plenty of evidence to support it, and none which counts against. This is the logical character of an inference, and there are numerous other examples which could be cited of equally well established connections such that when B occurs we are justified in asserting that A has occurred to cause B.

This is the model upon which many theories, and much unreflective talk of the expressiveness of actions, dance movements, and works of art in general, are based. We perceive B, the overt physical action or work of art, and infer from it to A, the inner emotion which was the cause of it. Such theories certainly have the advantage of simplicity. Unfortunately they also have the disadvantage of being false, or rather not so much false as nonsensical. A little probing soon shows that the apparent clarity and simplicity is specious.

Perhaps it should be said at the outset, to avoid misunderstanding, that the argument which follows does not attempt to deny that physical movement, actions and works of art can express emotions. In many cases the arts undoubtedly do have a close connection with emotions, and physical actions can express feelings. The argument is intended to expose the deeply ingrained fallacies inherent in this particular, very commonly held notion of the *nature* of the connection between emotion and action or art. For, paradoxically, a consequence of this theory is that it would be unintelligible to talk of the expression of emotions, whether in life-situations or in art. Furthermore, in the way it is usually, and very naturally understood, this traditional theory of the emotions, as I shall call it, underlies and leads to much of the muddled and mystical writing and thinking which is so prevalent in discussion of the arts, and especially the art of movement.

Well, what is wrong with the traditional theory, or dualism, as it is usually called? There are several interrelated fallacies, of which the two most important are:

(a) An inadequate theory of the relationship between mind and body, of which the traditional theory of the emotions is a species.

(b) An inadequate theory of meaning in language.

We shall show first that the traditional view is radically misconceived, and then go on in section B to see how a mistaken theory of meaning seems to lead imperceptibly and almost inexorably to mistaken beliefs about the mind and emotions.

It should be said that most of those who talk or write in a way which reveals what I have called the traditional view, do not *explicitly* hold that theory, for they do not trouble to spell out its consequences. The connection between inner feelings and outer expression is left vague. But, usually, if pressed to an explanation, they tend to suggest that there is an inferential connection of the sort outlined.

Let us look more closely at the suggestion that an inference is possible in this sphere. The suggestion is that we work backwards from the external, publicly observable physical expression in movement to the internal, private, mental emotion of which it is an expression, by causal inference. But compare this with the case of the windmill.[1] I was able to infer from seeing the windmill sails turning that there was a wind blowing, and that the wind was the cause of this movement of the sails. But it is important to notice that the justification of *this* inference depends upon such factors as my having been in a position where I could both directly experience the wind blowing and at the same time see the sails going round. While standing outside I might feel the

---

[1] For simplicity we shall confine our attention to the factor of our experience of the concurrence of wind and turning sails. However, we should remember that the position is very much more complex than that. It has been said that we are burdened by a mass of cognition. One inevitably brings to any particular case a considerable amount of background knowledge. Such knowledge in this case would include one's own, and others' experience of other causal connections, other effects of wind and like forces etc. Thus Strawson (1966) says:

"Concepts of objects are necessarily compendia of causal laws. They carry implications of causal power or dependence."

wind violently blowing my hair, I might see the trees bending and swaying, the leaves scattering. At the same time I notice that the sails of the windmill are spinning rapidly. On another occasion I might have to moisten a finger and hold it up in order to detect a light breeze, while concurrently noticing that the sails are barely managing to heave themselves round. I frequently experience directly this concurrence of the two events—the sails turning and the wind blowing. It is also the experience of other people. A considerable weight of evidence accrues that when and only when the wind is blowing the sails turn. Furthermore, though I am now entirely justified in assuming, from the shelter of my study, that there is a wind blowing solely on the evidence of the turning sails, and without directly feeling the force of the wind, it is always open to me to check the correlation, by going outside to confirm that the wind really is blowing.

How different this is from the inference upon which the traditional dualist theory is based, for in that case the only evidence we have for the existence of an emotion is the external physical behaviour of the person who is feeling the emotion. Spectators cannot possibly get "behind" the external movement to find out what inner emotion it is expressing, for the evidence is occurring in the mover's mind, and the theory insists that minds are inaccessibly private. No one else can know directly what is going on in someone's mind. Thus emotions are inviolably concealed behind walls far more effective as guardians of privacy than the strongest walls ever built, for they are *logically* impenetrable. It is as impossible, on this theory, to know directly what is going on in someone else's mind as it is to draw a triangle with four sides.

This is in sharp contrast to the inference in the case of the windmill where there were two separately identifiable and directly verifiable events, the turning of the windmill sails, and the blowing of the wind. Experience has shown us that there is a regular correlation between them, and it is precisely this experience which allows us legitimately to claim to know that the wind is blowing, even though we may be unable to feel or hear it directly, but can only see, through a window, the turning sails.

In the case of emotions we not only do not, but logically cannot have a similar situation. For, it is said, only the performer of an emotionally expressive movement can have direct knowledge of the emotion he is feeling. Observers cannot verify their assumed correlation by direct access. So there is an insuperable difficulty about this supposed inference. According to the traditional view, it is possible to observe only one event, the physical movement, yet we are supposed simply to assume the concurrence of the other event, the emotion, without any independent evidence of its existence whether on this or on any previous occasion.

Consider another example. Suppose that I live in a semi-detached house. One day, late in the afternoon, I hear a rattle as of crockery etc., and this is accompanied by sounds of laughter, chatter and occasional shrieks of excitement. I may well be justified in inferring that there is a children's tea party going on in the neighbouring house. The justification for my inference will be stronger, if, for example, I know that there are children living next door who love parties and who have indulgent parents, and that subsequent to my having heard such sounds on previous occasions I confirmed that the children were having parties.

The two events, the sounds I can hear in my house, and the tea party next door, are separately identifiable and directly verifiable. I can hear the sounds without seeing the tea party. I can also, if I am deaf, or if I use effective ear-plugs, watch the tea party without hearing the sounds. Again, I can actually go and check the validity of my inference. I can go and see whether in fact the sounds which I can hear are caused by a tea party on this occasion too.

The situation is very different in the case where we attribute expressiveness to a physical movement. Observers can see the physical movement easily enough, but how can they find out that it is caused by the particular emotion of which it is said to be an expression? Indeed, how can one be certain that it is caused by an emotion at all? It could be merely fortuitous, perhaps a reflex action. It is not possible to confirm directly that there is a correlation with an emotion, as one could confirm directly the occurrence of the tea party on the evidence of the sounds coming from the adjacent house. What is worse, from the point of view of the credentials of the inference, in the case of emotions we have *never* been able to verify that particular emotions, hidden in the necessarily private recesses of another's mind, cause particular physical expressions of them. Thus, as observers, we are in a very weak position for proposing even a superficially plausible hypothesis of causal inference.

In short there are two conditions which have to be fulfilled in order to justify our making a legitimate inductive inference:

(a) It must be logically possible to perceive directly the entity or event whose existence one is inferring indirectly.

(b) In order to have adequate grounds for the inference one must on previous occasions have been directly aware of the same kind of entity or event or one must have good evidence that others have had this experience.

In the case both of the windmill and of the tea party these conditions were fulfilled. But in the case of the theory of emotional expression which we are considering, neither of these conditions can be fulfilled. For it is a tenet of the theory that emotions are ineluctably private and inaccessible to direct observation.

Referring to the etymology of "expression" we took the example of squeezing water from a sponge. We can now see why it is significant that it is the same water which emerges as was contained in the sponge prior to the squeezing. For it is easy to confirm that it is the same water. One could, for example, use coloured water to check that the water which is soaked up by the sponge remains in it until squeezed out. But in the case of emotional expression there is no such experiment which can be performed. There is no way of checking that the emotion which is "in" a person's mind is the same as that which is said to be indicated by his overt physical actions.

It might be objected that the position is not as bad as has been suggested, for there is one important exception which has so far been overlooked. There is, it might be said, one way in which it is possible to discover that particular physical movements are expressive of particular emotions, and that is in one's own case. The theory allows, indeed it insists, that we have direct access to our own minds by introspection, thus in my own case I can confirm by direct experience that there is a correlation between my expressive movement and a particular emotion. Furthermore, I have often had this experience in the past. Hence the two conditions for a legitimate inference appear to be fulfilled. By introspection I have discovered that expressive movement M is caused by, or at least preceded by and an expression of, emotion E. For example, I may have discovered that a feeling of extreme sadness induces in me a tendency to weep, i.e., that overt weeping behaviour expresses the internal mental emotion of extreme sadness. Hence, it might seem that I can assume that when other people are seen to be weeping they too are feeling extreme sadness. My confidence in this assumption is based upon my own direct experience.

There are some difficult problems inherent in this way of talking, some of which we shall examine later. At this point it will suffice to notice that even if we accept the assumptions on which this objection is based, it won't do at all. For on apparently simple empirical grounds it proposes an unjustifiable generalisation on the flimsiest evidence. According to the objection, in my own case only I notice this correlation of extreme sadness and weeping behaviour. Yet on the basis of only this one case I make the rash generalisation that everyone else is the same. It may be that my behaviour is extremely eccentric, that it correlates oddly or not at all with my inner emotion. No reputable scientist would construct a theory on the basis of only one test case.

How, on this theory, do I know that other people who are weeping are not thoroughly enjoying themselves?[1] All that is observable is the external behaviour. Even if in my own case I can discover that this always indicates an inner emotion of extreme sadness, how can I be certain that this is true of other people? According to the theory it is impossible to discover directly what others are feeling. So that if, to know what a movement is expressing, we need to delve into the hidden recesses of another's mind, the obvious fact is that we shall never be able to discover what any behaviour expresses, not even in such extreme cases as that of weeping behaviour. Any sort of behaviour could be expressing any sort of emotion. In comes a gentleman with fiery red hair, his eyes blazing, his lips trembling. He swears and shouts, alternately shaking his fist and crashing it violently on the table. "Well, now," we muse to ourselves, "I wonder whether he is feeling calm and contemplative today." According to the theory the only way to find out is to ask him. A road accident victim, evidently badly injured, lies groaning in the road. On this theory it would be possible that his groans and writhing were expressing contentment or great joy.

To relate these issues to aesthetic expression in movement, consider the following example. In the repertoire of the Alvin Ailey Dance Theatre during a recent visit to London was a solo dance entitled *Adagio For a Dead Soldier*. The dancer performed exquisitely a writhing, contorted series of movements expressing the ineffable agony of eternal loss. On the traditional view such a dance could have been expressing the gaiety of a Mozart Rondo. For if the meaning of the dance, that which it is expressing, is given by the necessarily private, inner emotion of the dancer, which accompanies or immediately precedes the movements of the dance, then for all

---

[1] I am ignoring, of course, cases of weeping for joy, or because of peeling onions etc. Such cases are obviously irrelevant to the argument. The weeping behaviour which concerns us is that which we all normally recognise without difficulty as expressing extreme sadness.

the observers know to the contrary the supposedly grief-expressing movements may in fact be expressing some quite different emotion. There is, on this view, no way of telling what is being expressed in the movements of the dance.

This is not to say that when we are watching expressive behaviour we are considering only the immediately observable anatomical and physiological phenomena. We obviously can and do know in most cases, at least to some extent, what is being expressed in certain human actions. We know that weeping behaviour expresses sadness, that the writhing road accident victim is suffering pain, and that the dancer is, to put it crudely, expressing an extreme agony of grief. Yet the irony is that we could not know any of these things if in order to discover what actions express it really was necessary to delve into the logically private recesses of a person's mind in order to verify directly the emotion which caused them. Thus, so far from solving or explaining anything about the expressiveness of behaviour, the traditional theory makes it impossible to connect behaviour with emotions.

· Two more objections might occur, at this point, to anyone unfamiliar with this argument. First, one might object that it seems to be denying facts frequently confirmed by everyday experience. For the argument seems to be casting doubt on the notion of a private, inner, mental sphere where emotions occur. Yet it is obvious, and common knowledge, that no one else can know what one is feeling, that only I can really know my own emotions.

Well of course one cannot deny the obvious fact that very often another person cannot tell what one is feeling. Any theory of the emotions must be adequate to this fact of human experience, but we should be careful not to exaggerate the position. For it is also true that very often other people know better than I do what I am feeling, as in the case of the man who bangs his fist on the table and roars, "I tell you I am not angry!" People sincerely deny that they are jealous, or in love, or afraid, when we know very well from our observation of their behaviour that they are in fact experiencing these emotions. In *Hamlet* the player queen, no doubt believing herself sincere, professes rather profusely her eternal love for the player king. But the onlooking Gertrude observes, "The lady doth protest too much methinks." Self-deception of this sort is by no means rare, so that on some occasions the onlooker is more aware of the character of an emotion than the person experiencing it. A great part of psycho-therapeutical treatment consists of the psychiatrist's attempting to induce his patient to recognise and accept the true character of the emotions he feels. It is the patient's inappropriate interpretation of and reaction to his own emotional states which largely constitute his distress. In an important sense he fails to understand his own emotions. And even in cases where, aware of their character, we do keep emotions to ourselves, we should recognise that the ability to do so is an acquired ability. The younger the child the less is he able to keep his emotions to himself, as one can readily confirm. Infants notoriously, and at some cost to our patience at times, cannot restrain their emotional reactions. So that even if the misleading model of inner and outer is retained, it would appear to be more appropriate to suggest that the proper direction of travel is the opposite to that proposed by the traditional theory. Instead of emotions being naturally inner and overflowing into outer physical actions, it would seem to be more accurate to say that emotions begin in childhood as outer, spontaneous physical reactions, and only later become inner as the child learns self-control.

Though one certainly would not wish to deny that the person who feels an emotion has a different way of knowing about it from anyone else, this is not to say that he is the only person who can know that he is feeling an emotion. And, significantly for our enquiry, it is not to say that he is the only person who can recognise *what* emotion he is feeling. When it comes to recognising the character of his feelings he may well be in no better a position than someone observing him.

Just as, despite my protestations to the contrary, you may more accurately recognise the character of my emotion than I do, so I might surprise myself. Though there is certainly a sense in which only I can feel the emotion, it is certainly not the case that I am always the best judge of what emotion I am feeling, until, perhaps, the true interpretation dawns on me. It may have been obvious to others for some time, yet the significance of certain sensations and aspects of my behaviour might strike me suddenly, as a revelation. Palpitations, dryness of throat and other relevant sensations in appropriate circumstances, as well as certain behavioural tendencies, previously ignored or misconstrued, might suddenly fall into an unmistakable pattern, inducing me to exclaim to myself, "Good heavens, I must be in love with her!"

The second objection is this. It might be pointed out that one can disguise one's real feelings and pretend to feelings which one does not in fact have. This is common enough. Indeed, such polite insincerity is only too common in "respectable" social intercourse. The existentialist philosopher Sartre (1969) characterises such socially acceptable pretence as "sliminess," and he warns against the handshake or smile which entices one into a spurious friendship which can drain away one's integrity to the point of an abnegation of self, a progressive decline in the ability to experience genuine vivid feeling.

So we can hide our real feelings and successfully pretend to other feelings. But this is far from lending support to the traditional theory of the emotions. The point has already been made that control of the emotions is acquired. There is the further point that we could not deceive other people about our emotional states unless for the most part people were able accurately to recognise the emotional states of others. Perhaps this can be more clearly appreciated by considering the analogous case of telling lies. It is possible to tell lies only in a community where truth-telling is the general practice. Similarly we can deceive others about our feelings only where it is generally true that people can recognise others' feelings. So far from undermining the case against the traditional view, this putative objection actually supports it.

The achievement so far is largely negative and necessarily so, for we cannot begin to think constructively until it has been convincingly shown that the old ideas are misguided. The peculiar difficulty of the theory, concerning the relationship of mind to body, which we have examined is that, though fundamentally misconceived, it is deeply ingrained, and still very commonly accepted by those who have not thought hard about it. Consequently, it generates confusion in a wide range of areas of thought, among which is our present concern with expression in movement and the arts generally. For a movement to express an emotion, it is not only not necessary but not possible that its expressive meaning should depend upon an inference to an emotional happening in an inaccessible region called a mind. Nevertheless, it is important not to misunderstand this by taking it as a denial that actions can express emotions whether in aesthetic or non-aesthetic contexts.

Perhaps the central point of the argument so far can be summed up, if somewhat enigmatically at this stage, by saying that the refutation of traditional dualism certainly does not imply that people do not have minds or experience mental events, but it does deny that it makes sense to regard minds and mental events as *things*. Obviously we can and do legitimately apply to people mental adjectives and descriptions, including attributions of emotional states, so in that sense there is nothing wrong with saying that there are minds. But, as we have seen, there are fatal objections to the belief that there are mysterious *things* called minds, and mental *things* such as sensations and emotions.

B:

MEANING

(1) The naming view

In any philosophical enquiry it is of the first importance not only to detect errors but to try to discover why we are led to making them. And perhaps the greatest single contributory factor to the common assumption that there must be such *things* as minds and emotions, is the second of the major mistakes mentioned above, namely that of an inadequate theory of meaning. This consists of two related misconceptions, neither of which can be adequately examined without the other:

(a) The assumption that the meaning of a word is what it names or stands for (the naming or denotational view).

(b) The assumption that what is named is a property common to the various instances in which the word is used correctly (the definitional view).

The meaning of a noun, for instance, is thought to be the object to which it refers, the meaning of a verb the activity to which it refers. In cases like "table", "moon", "Richard Nixon" and "playing tennis", this seems to present no problems. But not all cases are as straightforward as these, for sometimes a word refers to disparate phenomena. The word "game", for example, is applied to a wide variety of activities, many of which appear, on the face of it, to have nothing in common. There is a tendency, in such a case, to assume that the meaning of the word is to be found by discovering the underlying essence, which is fundamental to all the phenomena to which the word is applied. If we are asked what is the meaning of the word;

> "We feel that we can't point to anything in reply ... and yet ought to point to something." (Wittgenstein 1958. p.I.)

As an example of this tendency, let us imagine that we ask ourselves what is the meaning of "expecting", i.e. what it is to expect. We notice that the term is used in widely divergent ways, and there is no apparent conformity to a common feature or standard. Yet the word is meaningful, so we try to discover an underlying common feature, which is essential to the various instances of the use of the word. We observe what happens in cases where people are said to be expecting something, in order to try to locate this essential feature. It would be natural to consider first an obvious central case, such as a child, on his birthday, expecting the postman to bring parcels and cards. He is excited, restless, frequently runs to look out of the window, and jumps up at the sound of footsteps on the path. His thoughts are concentrated on the postman's arrival, and the evidence of his expectancy is abundant. Another central example is that of a bomb-disposal squad crouching behind cover, their fingers in their ears, faces screwed up, expecting an imminent explosion. Such cases seem to suggest some sort of intense mental activity which constitutes the essential meaning of expecting.

But now consider a very different case, in which a College tutor is sitting at home in an armchair, on a Saturday evening, reading *Alice Through the Looking Glass*. He is absorbed in the imagery of *Jabberwocky* and the perverse logic of Humpty Dumpty, yet, despite this, he is expecting a student for a tutorial at nine o'clock the following Wednesday. This case of expecting seems to have nothing in common with the previous ones, since the tutor is not thinking about the student at all. Yet the appointment is entered in his diary, and he has not forgotten it. Though this example differs greatly from the other two, it fulfils the requirements of expecting—for instance if anyone were to interrupt his reading to ask whether he would be free on Wednesday morning at nine, he would reply that he was expecting a student for a tutorial at that time. He might even fall asleep over the book, yet even then it could truly be said of him that he is expecting to see his student on Wednesday. So that the anxiety and intense preoccupation which were the conspicuous features of the child's expecting the postman and of the bomb-disposal squad, are obviously not necessary for a case to be one of expecting. This may well seem puzzling, for nothing can be discovered which is common to all three cases, yet we use the same word of each. It is tempting, nevertheless, to assume that there must be something in common, even though we cannot see what it is, for otherwise there seems to be no justification for our use of the word in each case. So, failing to find the common element which constitutes the expecting, we tend to postulate a transcendental, metaphysical element or event. Since we cannot *see* what is common we tend to assume that it must be an invisible mental event.

We are led to this conclusion by assuming that the word "expecting" must stand for something which is common to all the cases of expecting, if it is to be meaningful. This assumption reveals a failure to appreciate the range of possibilites of language. Naming is only one of the many functions of words, yet there is a pernicious tendency to regard it as the sole, or at least the pre-eminent function.

> We do here what we do in a host of similar cases: because we cannot specify any *one* bodily action . . . , we say that a spiritual (mental, intellectual) activity corresponds to these words.
> Where our language suggests a body and there is none: there, we should like to say, is a spirit. (Wittgenstein 1953, § 36).

Plato provides a good example of this way of thinking which, as we shall see, contributes largely to the confusion in discussion of the meaning of expressive movement. The Socratic Dialogues examine questions such as "What is knowledge, truth and justice?" Socrates is not satisfied with examples, he wants to locate the essence of the concepts—those conditions which are separately necessary and together sufficient to justify the legitimate use of the terms. Yet again and again he fails to define them comprehensively, since there are always exceptions to any proposed definition. Perhaps the best known example of this occurs in Book I of *The Republic,* where Socrates enquires about the meaning of justice. Several putative definitions are put to him, but to each he points out damaging objections. The result is a total failure to define the term, and Socrates muses sardonically on the strange fact that we use words like "justice" and "truth" without knowing what they mean.

To understand how this situation arises we need to uncover the assumptions about meaning which lead Socrates to this sceptical conclusion. They can be summarised in this way:

"To have meaning a term must name some element which is common to all the instances of its application. The nature of any concept can be determined only by discovering this common element. In the absence of any such common element or set of conditions, which is signified by the term in question, the term cannot be said to have any genuine meaning."

It can be seen how closely the meaning-as-naming view is connected with the definitional, or meaning-as-common-property view. It is assumed that to have meaning a word must signify something, but in the case of words such as "expecting", which are applied to widely diverse instances, it is difficult to see what could be signified. Hence it is thought that only by defining the concept, that is, locating the underlying essence which is common to all the instances of the application of the term, can we find a legitimate candidate for the signifying and therefore the meaning.

Plato takes over these presuppositions about meaning but he avoids Socrates' sceptical conclusion by moving to another realm. Socrates was unable to find the common element named by the term, so he concluded that it has no meaning. Plato agrees that the essence of a concept, named by the term, cannot be discovered in the normal way in which one discovers things, but he insists that such words as "truth" and "justice" do have meaning. It strikes Plato, as it would strike us, as implausible to suggest that such words, which are in everyday use, have no meaning. Hence, since he shares Socrates' presuppositions about the requirements for meaning, Plato continues to insist that there is a named essence even though it cannot be discovered by the normal methods of enquiry. According to Plato the essence, the common property signified by the term, is present even though it cannot be seen. It is a form which exists in an extra-terrestrial, transcendent order of being. Instances of the correct application of the term "true" are instances of the Form of Truth. Thus, for Plato, the meaning of a word is guaranteed by its signifying a common essence after all, even though it cannot be discerned in the normal way.

This shows how easily an enquiry into the meaning of a word or concept, when preconceptions about language misrepresent what can be counted as knowing the meaning of a word or concept, can lead to the postulation of other-wordly events. An exactly similar way of thinking underlies much mystical and confused talk and theorising about the expressiveness of movement. It may be said, for example, that a particular movement is expressive. This invites the question "What does it express?" The reply may be that the movement expresses sadness, but this immediately raises problems comparable to those facing Socrates and Plato. The movement has meaning which is given by the sadness it expresses, yet we cannot detect the sadness, as something distinct from the movement. Furthermore, some painting, poetry, novels and music also express sadness, and in the case of these art forms too, we can observe nothing but the respective physical media. We are convinced that their meaning is given by the sadness which they express, hence there is a tendency to think that each of these forms of art expresses an emotional state of mind which we call sadness. The movement, for example, is often said to be symbolic of the inner feeling of sadness, and it is this function of symbolism which is the meaning of the expressive movement. Yet the emotion is not something which we can see and point to, as we can see and point to its outward expression in physical movement and other art forms. So we tend to react rather as Plato did. Plato, presupposing that to have meaning a word must stand for something, and agreeing with Socrates that nothing observable could be found which it could stand for, postulated an invisible entity which it stood for, and which thus endowed the word with meaning.

There is a tendency to make similar assumptions about the meaning of "sadness" and, one might say, about the meaning of sadness. It is tempting to assume that actions and movements which are expressions of sadness, which have a sad meaning, are endowed with the character of sadness in much the same way as words are endowed with meaning in language, and that is by standing as a sign of something. Finding nothing observable signified by the word "sad", or symbolised by the movement which is expressive of sadness, we tend to assume not a Platonic celestial Form, but an equally unobservable inner emotion, hidden in the mind. The underlying assumption, in each case, which seems to impel us towards the conclusion that there must be such mysterious entities is the very natural and unquestioned assumption that the meaning of a word or of an expressive movement is an object. Just as Plato preserved his unquestioned assumption that meaning is an object by postulating the other-wordly realm of Forms, so there is a tendency to preserve the unquestioned assumption that meaning is an object by postulating a mystical place called the mind which "contains" in some inexplicable sense, mystical entities called emotions.

Analogously the meaning of sad movements is thought to

depend upon their symbolising inner emotions in the mind of the mover. The mind becomes a convenient, indeed a necessary, place in which to dump all the insoluble puzzles created by our distortedly limited notions about the meaning of words in language, and the meaning of emotionally expressive movements. The mind becomes a sort of meta-physical dustbin.

The cause of the trouble lies in the tenacious assumption that words like "mind", "emotion" and their cognates name things in the same way as words like "table" and "moon". And since we cannot point to minds and emotions as we can point to a table and the moon, we tend to think that minds and emotions are hidden, mysterious entities. To clear away the confusion we need to eradicate the misconception of taking the meaning of a word, or of an expressive movement, as something it stands for. We should take the use of a word as determining its meaning, since using it correctly manifests our understanding of that meaning. We are not, in using it, expressing something which lies behind it, any more than in performing an expressive movement a dancer is expressing something which lies behind, and gives light and colour to the movement.

B:

MEANING
(2) The definitional view

We need now to look more closely at the definitional view of meaning. It is commonly supposed that one can be said to know the meaning of a word only if one can define it. We have seen that Socrates considered that it was possible to determine the meaning of a general term, such as "justice", only if he could find the single element, or set of conditions, which was common to all the instances of its application. This assumption is still accepted without question, at least implicitly, by many if not most people. One is frequently asked to define one's terms, and a refusal or failure to do so is taken as tantamount to a confession that one does not know their meaning, i.e. that one does not know what one is talking about. Thus the definitional view can be seen to consist of two contributory assumptions:

(a) If a general term applies to several instances, its meaning consists in the possession by those instances of some common property or set of conditions.

(b) It is only if one is able to say what a term means, by citing the common property which it designates, that one can be said to understand the term.

What is required of a definition? Socrates' practice may be taken to illustrate what is still a prevalent, if implicit, demand for a very stringent requirement. It must be wide enough to encompass all the legitimate instances of the application of the term to be defined, yet it must not be so wide that it will allow in extraneous instances. To give an artificial example, if we define "yellow" as "coloured", this will certainly include all the relevant cases, since everything yellow is coloured, but it will also allow in many cases which are not yellow, such as red and green. So, as a definition, this would be too wide. Conversely, if we define "coloured" as "yellow" our definition is not wide enough, since there are many colours other than yellow.

This may seem very obvious, but before we can adequately consider the definitional view we need to be clear about precisely what is required of a definition. Paradoxically, most people are not at all clear about it, despite the fact that definitions are so frequently invoked to demand precision in the way other people use words. The implicit requirement is that a term is genuinely defined when and only when another term or set of terms is produced which is logically equivalent to it. An example of logical equivalence is the definition of a bachelor as an unmarried man. That a man is a bachelor logically implies that he is an unmarried man, and, conversely, that a man is unmarried logically implies that he is a bachelor. We can make the point schematically:

bachelor → unmarried man
unmarried man → bachelor
i.e. bachelor ⇌ unmarried man.

The implication holds both ways, thus the two terms are logically equivalent. Another way of putting the point is to say that in any context where "bachelor" appears, "unmarried man" could be substituted without any change of meaning.[1]

---

[1] There are contexts, for example quoted words, where it is not possible, without change of meaning, even to replace ' bachelor" by ' unmarried man".

However, most cases are not as simple as this. Most definitions require several conditions which are separately necessary and together sufficient for the concept in question. Thus a triangle can be defined as a plane figure bounded by three straight sides. We might list the necessary conditions of a figure's being a triangle as follows.

To be a triangle it is necessary:
(1) that it should be a plane figure
(2) that it should have three straight sides
(3) that it should be bounded by those sides

Each is necessary. A figure could not be a triangle if it lacked any one of these conditions. Together, but only together, these conditions are sufficient to guarantee that the figure is a triangle. Again we have logical equivalence. Wherever the term "triangle" appears we could substitute "plane figure bounded by three straight sides", and though the latter would be a relatively clumsy formulation, there would appear to be no change of meaning, at least in most cases. So if logical equivalence is required of a definition, then we can claim to have defined a triangle. Presumably Socrates and the most rigorous modern definist would be content with this as a definition. But notice that even this paradigm of a definition depends upon underlying non-collusive agreement about the meanings of the words which are used in the definition. It has to be assumed that people understand what is meant by "plane", "bounded", "straight" etc. It is a point of some significance that if a definition had to be given before we could understand the meaning of *every* word, then we should never be able to understand the meaning of *any* word. We should be launched upon the dizzy frustration of a vicious infinite regress. Every word in the definition would itself have to be defined in words each of which would have to be defined in words each of which would have to be defined . . . , and so on *ad infinitum*. So to give a definition already presupposes an understanding of the meanings of the words which comprise the definition.

What is more, the ability to recognise a definition as correct, or to raise counter-examples to it, already pre-supposes that one knows the meaning of the term to be defined before the definition is produced.

Even leaving aside these problems, we are unable in most cases to produce definitions of the words we use, though we are well aware of their meanings. For example, we are unable to define the primary colours. But our inability to produce a term or set of terms which is logically equivalent to "yellow" does not prevent our understanding and using it correctly. And we certainly learned its meaning without being given a definition. "Yellow" could be defined as "coloured", or more precisely as "one of the primary colours". But though this might well be useful to clear up a failure of under-standing in a particular case (and this typically is the *point* of a definition), it will not, as we have seen, satisfy the stringent requirement of logical equivalence which is implicit in the demand made by most people on a definition.

Consider two more examples. A knife may be defined as an instrument for cutting. But, though it may be a necessary condition of an object's being a knife that it be an instrument used for cutting, this is not a sufficient condition. Other objects, such as a saw, are used for cutting. The definition is too wide, and thus allows in extraneous objects. An example which errs in the opposite direction is that of the frequently proffered definition of "aesthetic appreciation" as "apprecia-tion of the beautiful". It may well be true that when we consider something as beautiful we are considering it aesthetically, i.e. that appreciation of beauty is sufficient to indicate aesthetic appreciation. But many objects which are normally considered objects of aesthetic appreciation are not normally considered beautiful. So that, though appreciation of the beautiful may be a sufficient condition, it is not a necessary condition of aesthetic appreciation. The proposed definition is too narrow. It excludes some genuine cases of aesthetic appreciation. Now of course this does not show that we do not understand the meaning of "knife" and of "aesthetic". What it does show is that there is something wrong with the assumption that we can be said to understand the meaning of a term only if we can define it, when, as is usually the case, the implicit demand on a definition is the stringency of logical equivalence.

Socrates clearly demonstrates that most terms which become subject to philosophical enquiry cannot be strictly defined. Though we should probably want to agree with him about this, most of us would not want to agree with his conclusion that we do not therefore know the meaning of such terms as "truth", "true", "justice", "just" etc. We may not have a full grasp of the meaning of such terms—a full-scale philosophical analysis of the concepts concerned may be required for that. But we regularly use such terms in everyday conversation, and, by and large, we understand them. In many cases, particularly of complex concepts, proposed definitions will be found to fail on at least one of two counts. They will, on examination, prove to be either

(a) false, i.e. they will be susceptible to counter-examples.
or
(b) vacuous, i.e. the apparent explanatory value of the definition will turn out to be specious.

By way of illustration let us consider more fully an example given above. The Oxford Dictionary gives, as a definition of "aesthetic", "Belonging to the appreciation of the beautiful". If we take the word "beautiful" in its normal sense, which would be the natural way to take it, then this definition can easily be shown to be false. For there are many objects which are normally considered primarily from an aesthetic point of view which are ugly or even distinctly abhorrent. Consider, for example, most of the paintings of Francis Bacon, those of Goya in the black period, some of Picasso, for instance *Guernica*. Consider Shakespeare's so-called horror play *Titus Andronicus*, Samuel Beckett's *Endgame*, some of Ingmar Bergman's films, for example *The Shame*, and Franz Kafka's *Metamorphosis*. These works of art, and there are many more one could cite, are the objects primarily of aesthetic interest, but they would not, in any normal sense of the word, be considered beautiful. Such counter-examples appear effectively to refute the putative definition of "aesthetic".

But proponents of the definition, in order to preserve it from such counter-examples, sometimes propose a plausible argument which would go something like this:

> "Of course it is true that the works of art you have mentioned above, and many more, are not beautiful in the normal sense of that word, i.e. roughly the opposite to "ugly". But the peculiar kind of beauty which is manifested in works of art is not of this kind. It is a unique sort of beauty which *is* present in even the works of art you have cited, for example the savage paintings of Francis Bacon. One should not confuse beauty in this particular sense, with the ordinary sense of the term."

Well, this certainly saves the definition but at great cost, for now we find that the definition is of no help. We wanted to know what "aesthetic" meant and we were told it meant "Belonging to the appreciation of the beautiful". Now we are told that "beautiful" is not to be understood in its normal sense. So obviously we shall want to know precisely what is the sense in which we are to understand it, and if we press hard enough the likelihood is that we shall be told, in effect anyway, that we are to understand "beautiful" in a special aesthetic sense. So the definition, under this interpretation, turns out to be vacuous. For to know what "aesthetic" means we apparently need to know first what is meant by "beautiful in a special aesthetic sense". But it was the meaning of "aesthetic" which the definition was supposed to elucidate in the first place, so the whole apparatus of the definition has simply deferred, rather than solved, the problem. Wittgenstein (1953, § 217), commenting on this sort of situation, says:

> Remember that we sometimes demand definitions for the sake not of their content but of their form. Our requirement is an

architectural one; the definition a kind of ornamental coping that supports nothing.

It does seem strange that we are so often satisfied with definitions which, after a little probing turn out to have little or no explanatory value. In such cases an "explanation" given in definitional form appears to have an effect comparable to "medicinal" coloured water. Doctors know well enough that some people can be satisfied only with one particular *form* of cure. Such patients have a preconception that to be cured necessarily involves taking medicine. So even when a doctor recognises that a particular ailment is not susceptible to any known medicinal treatment, and perhaps will, in any case, soon fade away quite naturally, he may prescribe coloured water in a medicine bottle. This may be the only way to convince the patient that he really is being cured.

Problems similar to those we encountered in the case of "aesthetic" will become apparent if we try stringently to define many other terms. An example is "moral" and its cognates. It is notoriously difficult, as one may readily confirm by consulting the literature, to locate the subject matter of both morality and aesthetics. It is worth noting, too, in support of the suggestion that definitions are often more of a formality than positively explanatory, that in many cases we have more difficulty in understanding the terms used in the definition than we would have with the term to be defined in the first place. Kennick (1965) gives an amusing example. Discussing Clive Bell's definition of Art as Significant Form, he remarks that, quite apart from the question of the validity of the definition, most of us would find it much easier to pick out works of art from a heterogeneous collection of objects in a warehouse than we would find it to pick out those objects which manifest Significant Form. The point is that the notion of Significant Form is more obscure than that of Art of which it was proposed as an explanation or definition.

A similar and more topical example is provided by the recent attempts in Britain to clarify the law on pornography or obscenity. Defendants in courts of law are accused of producing or selling obscene publications. Not surprisingly, in such cases, trials and appeals hinge on the meaning of "obscenity". As the law stands in Britain "obscene" is defined as "tending to deprave and corrupt". However, as quickly and frequently becomes apparent, there is as much difficulty about deciding whether a publication depraves and corrupts as there is about deciding whether it is obscene. This is a classic example of a definition which is, in effect, an ornamental coping stone, providing no substantial support.

A well-known barrister recently interviewed on radio conceded that the definition in law, as it now stands, is inadequate, but he confidently asserted that it would be a relatively easy matter to rectify this inadequacy simply by producing a more accurate, yet still concise, definition of "obscene". The learned barrister would appear to be far too optimistic. The hope of rectifying the lack of clarity in the law by more accurate definition is illusory as it is based upon a confusion. Quite apart from the general difficulties for definitions which we have examined, this one seems to be trying to define an evaluative concept in non-evaluative terms.

Wittgenstein (1953, § 66) challenges the assumptions on which the definitional view is based by showing that there need not necessarily be anything in common when the same word is applied to several different instances. He proposes the expression "family resemblances" to characterise the complex relationships which one might discover if one examined the ways in which general words are used. He asks us to consider, for example, the proceedings which we call "games":

"What is common to them all?—Don't say 'There must be something common, or they would not be called "games"—but *look and see* whether there is anything common to all.—For if you look at them you will not see something that is common to *all*, but similarities, relationships, and a whole series of them at that. To repeat: don't think, but look!"

Wittgenstein warns us not to think because of the danger of approaching the enquiry with a preconceived notion of what it is for a word to have meaning, rather like the patient who goes to his doctor with a preconceived idea of what it is to be offered a cure. We are enjoined to examine the problems with an open mind, rather than approaching the situation, albeit inadvertently, with a ready-formed theory of what it is for a word to have meaning.

Wittgenstein goes on:

"Look for example at board games, with their multifarious relationships. Now pass to card-games; here you find many correspondences with the first group, but many common features drop out, and others appear. When we pass next to ball-games, much that is common is retained, but much is lost.—Are they all 'amusing?' Compare chess with noughts and crosses. Or is there always winning and losing, or competition between players? Think of patience. In ball games there is winning and losing; but when a child throws his ball at the wall and catches it again, this feature has disappeared . . . And the result of this examination is: we see a complicated network of similarities overlapping and criss-crossing: sometimes overall similarities, sometimes similarities of detail."

He suggests the name "family resemblances" because:

"the various resemblances between members of a family: build, features, colour of eyes, gait, temperament, etc. etc. overlap and criss-cross in the same way.—And I shall say: 'games' form a family." (§ 67).

He anticipates an objection by someone who is still under the influence of the definitional view:

"But if the concept 'game' is uncircumscribed like that, you don't really know what you mean by a 'game'."

Wittgenstein replies to his imaginary questioner:

"When I give the description: 'The ground was quite covered with plants'—do you want to say I don't know what I am talking about until I can give a definition of a plant?" (§ 70)

It was suggested above that the definitional view consists of two contributory assumptions. In relation to the former, we can now see that when a general term is used this does not necessarily imply that there is anything common to the various instances of its use. And this simply dissolves the latter assumption, since, if there is no common feature, we obviously cannot say what it is.

Wittgenstein's notion of family resemblances is salutary in drawing attention to the fact that there is often no one feature or set of conditions common to the instances of application of a general word. This is particularly helpful in counteracting the danger of assuming that a word has meaning only if it can be defined. However, a cautionary note should be added, for there is an opposite danger of taking over the family resemblances model too liberally and too easily. This is a danger to which some of those who claim to be followers of Wittgenstein tend to succumb. It is misleading to assume that the family resemblance model of meaning is a universal panacea, conveniently applicable to any concept which proves to be somewhat elusive. For example, one sometimes encounters the rather facile assumption that art is a family resemblance concept. Yet it is, at any rate, not obvious on a superficial examination. It is easily overlooked that it is possible to claim a resemblance or connection of some sort between almost any two objects, perhaps because they are both in the world, or are both physical objects, or even because they have both been thought about. Presumably a stronger resemblance than any of these would be required by proponents of family resemblances. But the nature of the resemblance is left unclear, or even, more usually, presupposed. It could, for instance, be reasonably claimed that some examples of art appear to bear a closer resemblance to some examples of games than to other examples of art. Consider a competitive music festival. A group of musicians, perhaps a choir or a string ensemble, might be competing against other groups of musicians. On what basis do we decide that the model of family resemblances justifies our referring to such activities as "music" or "art" rather than "games"? It could surely be plausibly argued that this situation bears an equally close resemblance to competitive team games.

This is not to detract from the *point* of Wittgenstein's introduction of family resemblances, which is to expose the fallacy inherent in the common tendency to demand definitions. He was trying to expose the fallacy of the assumption that to have meaning a general word must signify an accurately specifiable number of properties common to the instances of its application. Unfortunately, contrary to Wittgenstein's expressly stated intention to encourage people to think for themselves, (1953, Preface), his remarks are sometimes taken over as a *substitute* for thinking.

B:

MEANING

(3) Variants of the definitional view

There are some variants of the definitional view of which we should be aware. One of the commonest is frequently unrecognised because it is surreptitiously and often inadvertently incorporated into apparently innocuous questions. These questions are of the form "What is X?", where X refers to a complex phenomenon or set of phenomena. The very form of the question is tendentious, in that it seems to impose certain limits, in advance, to the answer which can be given to it. Such questions already encapsulate certain presuppositions with which we may not want to agree, yet, if we are not careful, we may find ourselves forced into a position of at least appearing to accept them if only by implication. An obvious example is the demand for a clear yes-or-no answer to the question. "Are you still cheating in exams?" Even if one answers "No," there is an implication that one used to cheat in exams. The only way to answer accurately in such a case, i.e. without accepting the implications, is to reject the question in that form. Questions of this sort, though more subtly loaded, are sometimes used by politicians and lawyers, among others, to manoeuvre people into embarrassing positions. For example, a Conservative Member of Parliament, interviewed on television about the contentious issue of whether Britain should sell arms to South Africa, was asked, at the conclusion of the interview to give a brief unequivocal answer to the question, "Are you, then, in favour of Britain's supplying to the South African Government arms which could be used to kill black Africans?" This was a disingenuous attempt to impose limitations on his answer. He had been asked to be brief, but to give a brief reply to the question posed in that form would have put him in an unfair position. He would be unable to say, for example, that it was not a matter of killing black Africans, but rather of honouring the Simonstown Agreement, of augmenting trade, of countering the Russian threat in the Indian Ocean and of improving the lot of black Africans by means of more amicable relations with the South African Government. Yet if he declined to give a plain yes-or-no answer he might well give the impression of prevaricating.

This is, of course, neither to support nor to condemn the view which he held, but to expose a tendentious question. However, in passing, it may be worth adding that though politicians in general may be notoriously adept at evasive replies, we should not simply assume that their refusal to give plain answers always constitutes shifty equivocation.

These are fairly obvious examples, but some questions conceal their implications much more effectively, so that often the questioner himself is unaware of them. Many questions of the form "What is X?" are a species of this genus. We need to be aware of this danger, for aesthetics is one area of enquiry among many in which vacuous and mystical theories are proposed as answers because of a failure to recognise this sort of tendency in the questions.

Consider an example which we have already examined briefly, the problem of defining "aesthetic". This problem could be, and usually is, posed in the form of the question "What is aesthetics?" This question looks, superficially, like the question "What is a bachelor?" or "What is a triangle?"

Such questions as these last can be answered by providing nice, tidy definitions. The question "What is aesthetics?" has a similar *form,* so we tend to feel obliged to try to provide an equally crisp, compendious answer. But the *content* of the question this time, its subject matter, is much more complex. To see this, compare the variety of objects which we call triangles with the enormously greater variety of objects which are or can be of aesthetic interest. So, failing to appreciate this difference, we are at a loss to provide an answer. This is largely because we have too restricted a notion of what it is to be an answer. We tend to think that only a concise yet comprehensive statement can be regarded as an answer and since we cannot find one on this occasion, we may well have an uneasy feeling that our knowledge is deficient. Yet, in fact, our failure to provide this sort of answer may be good evidence that our knowledge of the relevant issues is greater than that of the person who provides one, for, in such a case as this, the demand for a simple answer is a demand for a false answer.

This tendency to assimilate questions to the single model of those which are in effect demands for definitions appears to have contributed largely to some of the misguided attempts, which are often encountered, to characterise art briefly. To ask oneself "What is art?" seems to impel one in this direction, consequently there are statements such as "Art is Expression" (Croce) and "Art is Significant Form" (Clive Bell). Such answers are good examples of definitions provided more for their form than for their content, for, taken as descriptive definitions, they seem to have very little, if any, explanatory value. "Art is Expression," as it stands, is obviously too wide, since there are many forms of expression which are not art. In the case of "Art is Significant Form" we shall want to know in what way art is significant and to whom. We already seem to be heading towards vacuous circularity, rather like that of the proposed definition of the aesthetic in terms of the beautiful. This is not to suggest that such definitions of art should necessarily be summarily dismissed. If they are to be understood as descriptive definitions, like that of the triangle, then they are indeed of little or no value. However, it seems much more likely that they should be understood as persuasive definitions, i.e. in effect, as proposals as to how one should look at art.[1]

A similar example is "What is dance?" Here again those who attempt to answer the question tend to feel under some pressure to try to find the essence, the single feature which is distinctive of dance. There is no obvious candidate, since it shares features with various other activities. So, assuming unwittingly that a genuine characterisation of dance must somehow be of the same form as the compact definition of a triangle, theorists have often produced what turn out to be merely nominal answers, often couched in eulogistic mystery. Many examples can be found in the literature on dance, such as:

> The dance is a symbolic form which reveals the creator's inner vision. (Hawkins 1964).

> ... dance, itself an expression of organised organic and bodily rhythm, must be considered as an extension of emotional and intellectual rhythmic form, projected into and through movement. (H'Doubler 1957).

> Dance ... is itself an instrument for a glorious and effective message of spiritual affirmation, realisation, and victory. It is the symbol of unified, harmonised and integrated life. (St. Denis 1941).

Another question which is misleading in this way, and which for that reason often puzzles students and teachers of physical education, is the question, "What is the difference between Modern Educational Gymnastics and Modern Educational Dance?" It is easy to fail to notice the trap set by the tendentious singular in this question, which tends to suggest that the difference is to be found in the presence or absence

---

[1] For a discussion of the character of definitions of art and aesthetics see Kennick (1965), Weitz (1962) and Diffey (1973).

of some essential property in one type of activity or the other. We are already on the road to confusion.

"The decisive movement in the conjuring trick has been made, and it was the very one that we thought quite innocent." (Wittgenstein 1953, § 308).

The unnoticed yet decisive trick in this case is the singular form of the question.

Sometimes it is suggested that the difference lies in the fact that dance is an aesthetic activity. But, quite apart from the difficulty, for someone who holds a definitional view, about the meaning of "aesthetic," no one who has watched or performed gymnastics, whether Modern or Olympic, can doubt that aesthetic evaluation is relevant in these activities too. Sometimes a naïve answer is proposed in terms of location, i.e. it depends whether the activity takes place in a studio or a gymnasium. But obviously dance can be performed in a gymnasium, just as gymnastics can be performed in a studio. Sometimes even use of apparatus is suggested, but this won't do either, for one has seen ingenious dances composed by students using apparatus in a gymnasium.

This is not to say that there is nothing of value in these answers. Each fails as an answer only if we assume that an answer must be of a certain form, namely concise, comprehensive, decisive. Our puzzlement is caused by the conflicting strain on the one hand of feeling that we have to produce a definitional sort of answer, and on the other hand of appreciating that there are many and various issues involved which cannot be squeezed without distortion into such a restricted compass. Only when we have recognised and freed ourselves from the inhibiting preconception about the character of an answer can we begin to do anything like justice to the complexity of a comparison between dance and gymnastics, for we shall have to take account of many differences and many similarities.

Similar puzzles are engendered by questions such as "What is the purpose of Physical Education?" and "What is the value of Physical Education?" One encounters many questions formulated in this way. Again they are in the tendentious singular, which suggests a single, essential purpose or value. It seems far more likely, in view of the wide and increasing range of activities subsumed under the title "Physical Education," that we shall find a number of purposes and values. Little may be gained by arguing about which is the overriding one.

Other examples more directly relevant to our enquiry are "What is expressive movement?" "What· is emotion?" and "What is mind?" To ask for a plain answer to such questions is to ask for ten gallons of complexity to be contained in a pint jug of simplicity. Such questions tend to lead very easily to the idea that there must be mysterious mental entities, as we saw in the example of expecting which we considered earlier. The form of the question "What is imagination?" seems imperceptibly to suggest that we should look for a general faculty of imagination. Since this general faculty cannot be discovered, it is often assumed to be inaccessibly mental. But we should be looking in the opposite direction, at actual cases of imaginative performance, since the criteria for imaginative ability are particular to particular activities. So we should look at what it is to perform imaginatively in the separate activities of dance, mathematics, football, poetry and philosophy. The imaginative scientist is not necessarily an imaginative pianist.

A comparable question is, "What makes a dancer a great dancer?" or, generically, "What makes an artist a great artist?" Such questions are related to the gravely mistaken, though common, demand for general aesthetic criteria, for a single set of standards which can be applied indiscriminately across the whole range of the arts, from Giotto to John Cage, from Shakespeare to Martha Graham. Certainly, if one has sufficient knowledge one might well provide an answer to the question "What makes Margot Fonteyn, or Paul Taylor, or Ram Gopal a great dancer?" One might, too, be able to give a more general answer with respect to a particular school or mode of dance. For example, one might indicate certain levels of attainment of technical competence which would be *de rigueur* for any great dancer in the tradition of classical ballet. Yet attempts are made to give general answers of much wider scope. It is said, for instance, that a great dancer needs extraordinary physical dexterity, needs to be a master of technique, needs a highly developed sense of rhythm, etc. Which is to say almost nothing. It is like saying that a great footballer needs to be extraordinarily skilful with a football.

Another of the many disguises of the definitional tendency is to hide behind the word "real" or "really", particularly in questions. Thus, "What is the *real* meaning of art?" "What is the dancer *really* expressing?" Such questions seem to invite us to look for some underlying, essential quality. Professor Wisdom, in his lectures at Cambridge, used to say that when the words "real" and "really" are used in this way, there is often something fishy going on. It is a salutary warning.

The expectations of the questioner often determine, at least to some extent, the answer. A cricketer hits a six and the question is asked, "What did he *really* do?" Despite the implication in the question, there are various possible answers, for example, in terms of physics, psychology and physiology. Or we could reply, "He won the match," "He lost the ball," "He broke his bat," "He demoralised the bowler," "He broke the pavilion clock," "He split his trousers," and so on. We usually know how to answer because we know the sort of answer expected, and this can sometimes mislead us into thinking that there is a single correct answer. Similarly, the teacher may ask her students, "What was the really important thing about that movement?" The teacher already knows the sort of answer she wants and will be suitably gratified to receive the "correct" reply from her students. She will be correspondingly disappointed in the "unperceptive" students who noticed the "wrong" thing. But, despite the form of the question, there may not be only one important feature of the movement.

It is important to try to recognise the various guises of the definitional tendency as it appears in "What is . . . ?" questions since failure to do so leads almost inevitably to confusion. Yet people are so deeply imbued with the notion that the only way to answer such questions is to give a definition, that they tend to feel that pointing out the impossibility of answering *in that form* is somehow evasive or quibbling. But one cannot give a simple answer to a complex question, and despite their deceptively simple appearance, many questions in this form are complex questions.

Recognising hidden implications in this way may be compared with an aspect of playing a game such as squash or tennis. One has to try to detect the decisive movement in the conjuring trick in this sphere too. It is often the shot that was played before, like the presupposition in the question, which causes the present difficulty. One may be beaten again and again by a particular shot on a squash court. One seems unable to cope with it however hard one tries, yet one would often employ one's energy more effectively not by chasing the ball even more determinedly, but by asking oneself what it is about the preceding play which persistently put one in a disadvantageous position. The failure may be not so much one's inability to return this difficult shot as allowing one's opponent to place it in that awkward position in the first place. Yet players frequently misdirect their efforts in this way, and it sometimes takes time before one realises that one is making this very error oneself. In the same way one can sometimes find oneself in an incoherent position from which to try to return an answer, as a result of failing to notice that the question itself has manoeuvred one into that position.

Recourse to the dictionary appears to lend support to the tendency towards a definitional view of meaning. The meaning of a word is often regarded as something fixed and precisely delimited, and the dictionary a sort of rule book. But though dictionaries may be repositories of correct meanings, they do not legislate those meanings—on the contrary, they have to change, where necessary, to follow common usage. If most people, over a period of time, regularly use a word in a way which differs from the meaning given in a dictionary, then that is good evidence that its meaning has changed, or is changing. The compiler of the dictionary would have to take account of it. For example, to continue to insist that, in all instances of its use, "nice" still means "fine" as in "a nice distinction," rather than its more usual current, colloquial meaning of "agreeable," would be mistaken pedantry. Sometimes this dependence of meaning upon usage may be regrettable since a colloquial usage may progressively blur a distinction or offend against grammar. The increasing incursion into English of the misuse of "hopefully," is a good example. "Hopefully Hitler is dead," if it makes sense at all, means that though Hitler is dead, he is hopeful, but it is colloquially used to mean what would be more accurately expressed as "one hopes that," or "I hope that, Hitler is dead." What is meant in this case may be obvious, but sometimes ambiguity arises, as in "Hopefully Hitler is dying." Does this mean that one hopes that Hitler is dying, or that, despite the fact that he is dying, Hitler is hopeful? The misuse fails to make it clear. Nevertheless, it has to be accepted that it is people's normal usage of words which determines their meanings.

No one denies, of course, that dictionary definitions can often be useful, in spite of the fact that they do not usually attain the stringency of logical equivalence. Dissatisfaction about this lack of stringency often reveals a tendency to regard language as a sort of calculus, but this is to adopt a view of language which is inappropriately rigid, and therefore misleading. It does not matter to the compiler of the dictionary that many of his definitions, if carefully scrutinised, may be shown to be susceptible to counter-examples. He is satisfied if his definitions, by and large, explain how terms are used. To expect more precision than this is misguided, for meaning in language is not precisely delimited. Certainly there are cases where definitions, in the strict sense of logical equivalence, are valuable—this is true, for instance, of neologisms, in the sciences and in many other spheres, where it is helpful on grounds of economy to create terms whose meanings are exactly stipulated for a particular purpose.

There is one further point which should be made in order to avoid misunderstanding. We have been concerned to see that not all or even most word-meanings can be given by definitions, but this is not to say that clarity is unimportant. On the contrary, it is of the first importance to be clear about the meanings of our terms. The point is that we should resist the temptation to think that such clarity can be achieved only or primarily by definition. The meaning of a word is given by its use in a living, developing language, it cannot be understood when prised off its setting in a multi-coloured pattern and considered in isolation against a white background. And the same is true of the meaning of an expressive movement. Meanings, whether of words or of expressive movements, can be understood ultimately only in relation to a context. One can, of course, ask for the meaning of a single word in isolation, but that meaning is answerable to and derived from the uses of the word in various contexts. To consider how a word is used in the whole fabric of the language of which it is a constituent part is to consider its meaning.

We should try, then, to avoid or eradicate the tempting but misleading notion that in applying a general word to several instances we are marking the possession by those instances of something in common, a something named by and which gives meaning to the general word. This is where the definitional view and the naming view become closely connected. The example of expecting which we considered illustrated the puzzlement which can be created by assuming that there must be such a common element to be found. This assumption tends easily and naturally to lead to the belief in a mental process as the invisible common element. Similarly, as we have seen, it may be said that a movement expresses sadness—that is its meaning. And since sadness can be expressed in various ways it is easy to assume that there must be a common element named by the word "sadness," and symbolised by these various expressions. Thus there is a close analogy between the fallacy of meaning-as-naming in language, and the fallacy of construing expressive movement as a symbol or expression of an inner emotion.

Wittgenstein (1953 § 11) compares the meanings of words with the functions of the different tools in a tool box. To think that it is the function of every word to name is like thinking that it is the function of every tool to knock in nails. A hammer has that function, but a screwdriver, or chisel, or spanner has a different one. To assimilate the functions of all the various types of words in language to naming is as mistaken as to assimilate all the functions of tools to that of a hammer. Similarly one should beware of the tendency to assume that a movement is emotionally expressive only to the extent that it is symbolic of something else. Not all words name, not every expressive movement symbolises. We are satisfied that someone knows the meaning of a word if he can use it appropriately and we are satisfied that a dancer is a competent performer of her art only if she can employ her movement "vocabulary" appropriately. Consider a simple example of a symbolic movement, that of a closed fist as against an open hand. We should not be satisfied that the dancer knew its meaning if she used a closed fist in inappropriate contexts yet insisted that, for her, it symbolised an emotion which, despite appearances, was in fact entirely appropriate to those contexts. Meanings, whether of words or of movements, have to be answerable, in principle at least, to public criteria.

Paradoxically, the mistake of those who hold the traditional view is not a failure to have searched hard enough to discover emotions, but, in a sense, to have searched too hard. For emotions are there to be seen every day in the ordinary actions of people. If we cannot see them it is because we are looking in the wrong direction. A person's emotions are not other things, of a different kind from his body and bodily movements. We do not discover that someone is, for example, angry, by seeing a movement and *inferring* the anger, it is rather that we quite simply *see* that he is angry. The emotion is an inextricable part of the movement itself, it is not a separate event going on in the indiscernible regions of a person's mind. We fail to find the emotion of which the movement is expressive only if we try to probe beneath what is visible in order to reach the inner self, while all the time the emotional character we are seeking is lying on the surface, in the movement itself.

B:

MEANING

(4) Meaning and the traditional
theory of the mind

At first sight the suggestion that expressive meaning is a characteristic of the movement itself, rather than a reflection in that movement of an inner emotion at a deeper level, might seem implausible. For in that case, it might be objected, how can one account for the difference between a physical movement *simpliciter,* and a physical movement which expresses an emotion? This is an issue which we shall consider more fully later, but we can already begin to sketch in the broad outlines of it. The point can be illustrated by considering an illuminating distinction drawn by Aristotle, and contrasting this with Plato.[1] Aristotle speaks of form as the character of an object, and he distinguishes this from the material of which the object is made. It is already significant that he is thinking in terms of forms of objects, as against Plato's Forms. There is not, as there is for Plato, a Form of horses, separately existing over and above individual horses. It is rather that one discovers the form of horses by observing

[1] I am particularly indebted to Renford Bambrough for ideas from his lectures and writings which contributed to my formulation of this section. See especially his book on the philosophy of Aristotle (1963).

45

them. Aristotle is drawing our attention to the familiar distinction between the form, or shape of an object, and the material from which it is constructed. The hexagonal shape of a coffee table, for instance, is not something *additional* to the wood from which the table was constructed. The wood was not made into a table by bringing to it some other entity, since there are not two separate things, wood and a shape. It would not be ˙possible to destroy the table and retain the particular shape of it. It is rather that the table is wood *in* a particular shape.

Analogously we do not have physical movement and, added to it in some cases, an expression of emotion. Here, as in the case of the table, the problem is not one of relating two distinct, independent entities, as is so commonly believed by traditional theorists. A table is a unitary object of two aspects, shape and materials, and an expressive movement is a unitary movement of two aspects, the physical movement and the emotional expression. The physical movement incorporates the expression of emotion, it is that sort of movement in that sort of context. A dancer creating an expressive movement, expressing certain emotions in her movement, is not, or at least is not necessarily, doing two things, (a) performing certain physical movements, and (b) undergoing certain inner feelings. The expression is given, if at all (and that depends on the dancer's skill and sensitivity), in the movement itself, not by an inference to a something lying behind it, and called an emotion.

This is one aspect of the general problem of the relationship between body and mind. There are, it seems, on the one hand mental events, such as emotions, and on the other hand bodily events such as movements of the limbs or facial features. There has been a long and prolix debate throughout the history of philosophy about the connections between them. Thus it is easy to understand the common belief that body and mind are two distinct entities. One might, for example, ask oneself what is the difference between a living man and a dead body, and it would be plausible to suppose that the difference consists in the fact that something is missing from the dead body, which was present within the living man. The temptation to look at the problem in this way is, as we have seen, largely the result of a misconception about meaning which takes it for granted that all words including "living," "mind" and "emotion," name things. Furthermore, the question is another example of the tendentious singular, for to try to provide an answer to "What is *the difference* between a living man and a dead body?" is already to be launched on the slippery slope to dualism. In this form, the question suggests a single, essential difference, and since it cannot be detected in the normal way, there is a natural tendency to assume that it is an unobservable, mysterious entity called a mind, soul or spirit. The body which remains, we can see without any difficulty, so the difference is assumed to be something invisible which has departed.

But we can ask ourselves, instead, "What are the *differences* between a living man and a dead body?" This is much less likely to impel us towards a dualist position, for there are many differences. The dead body cannot see, hear, talk, move; its heart is not beating, it is not breathing, its brain is not functioning etc. The changed form of the question is more likely to allow us to see the situation in this light, and it therefore removes the temptation to believe in a metaphysical entity which was present in the living man, but which has now left his body.

Plato is a dualist, according to whom the soul departs from the body on death. Aristotle, on the other hand, regards the soul, or mind, as analogous to the shape of a body, and not as an additional entity. He illustrates his point in this way. If a man's eye is irreparably damaged we may say that he has lost the sight of that eye, and we are not tempted to assume in this case that there is a spiritual entity called "the sight" which has departed. We mean simply that the eye no longer performs the functions characteristic of a normally healthy eye. Yet we so often find it difficult to grasp this point where there is a loss of all the functions of a human body in death.

Consider the example of a jigsaw puzzle. What is the

difference between the haphazard assortment of pieces as they are tipped out of the box, and the completed picture of the Matterhorn? It does not consist in the addition of some entity in the latter case. Though we have the same number of pieces when the puzzle is correctly assembled, there is a considerable difference between it and the initial random heap, but it consists in a changed organisation of those pieces. The completed picture manifestly could not exist in the absence of the pieces that make it up.

The error committed by those who hold the traditional mind/body dualist view has been characterised by Ryle (1949) as a "category mistake". He gives the example of a foreign visitor who wishes to see Cambridge University, and is taken to see the colleges, the lecture rooms, the laboratories, the playing fields and the administrative buildings. If he is under a misapprehension analogous to that of the traditional theorist of the mind, he might, after his tour, ask this question. "It is very interesting to see the colleges, lecture rooms etc. but where is the University? That is what I really came to see." He is making a category mistake, since he assumes that the University is an entity different from, but in the same category as, the colleges and lecture rooms, and that just as he has been taken to see these, he can *also* be taken to see the University. His misapprehension is a failure to understand that in seeing the colleges and lecture rooms he *is* seeing the University. For the University is the organisation of all the constituent features which the visitor has seen.

Similarly, the mind is not a separate entity in, but an organisation of the body, and an emotionally expressive movement is not a movement in conjunction with an emotion, it is a particular organisation or pattern of movement which we recognise as emotionally expressive.

It is important to our enquiry to recognise the pervasive influence of the traditional, dualist, view about mind and body, and also to understand why it is so compelling. For it is at the root of most of the confused writing and talk about expressive meaning in the arts, and especially, perhaps, in the art of movement. On this view the meaning of an emotionally expressive movement, whether aesthetic or not, is left in the nebulous realm of inner feelings. At best this precludes both describing our own feelings and appreciating the feelings of others, since each is limited to his own feelings.

Some people recognise, albeit dimly in most cases, the incoherence of a merely contingent, inferential connection between outer physical movements and inner emotions. They realise that the only intelligible way to put the emotion into the movement is somehow to guarantee the relationship between them. For, if the connection between body and mind can, in general, be guaranteed we are restored to the position which obtains normally anyway, of being perfectly well able to understand what is expressed in human actions, at least in many cases. So these people often react in a way reminiscent of Plato. They suppose a connection which is guaranteed transcendentally, by a sort of pantheistic faith in the universal similarity of feelings and physical movements. Sometimes the creed goes to extravagant lengths, extending to all living organisms, and even to the movements of the heavenly bodies. The penalty for providing such a guarantee is heavy, for it has transferred the meaning of expressive movement to a celestial realm, with the consequence that it can no longer be intelligibly discussed, and the exchange of reasons for our differing interpretations of a particular dance performance becomes entirely out of place. We shall discuss this sort of theory more fully in section D (2).

Despite the difficulties inherent in the traditional view, our everyday talk is impregnated with it, but confusion does not necessarily, or even usually, ensue. We normally understand perfectly well what is meant by talk of the "inner spirit" revealed in a dance or painting. One is not suggesting that the motto "Mens sana in corpore sano", a healthy mind in a healthy body, be abandoned because of its philosophical unintelligibility. It would be mere sophistry in everyday speech to cavil at the great philosophical problem centred on the small word "in", for the motto is not normally understood in a way which creates such problems. Its function is to encourage stimulating and worthwhile activities of both an intellectual and a physical nature.

Of course there are, as Ryle (1949) and others have shown, insuperable problems about how a mind, spirit, or soul can be literally *in* a material body, but the point of our everyday use of this sort of phraseology is not normally vitiated by such problems. When we are told that someone hardly earns enough to keep body and soul together, we are not puzzled by the incoherence of the suggestion that a mysterious non-physical entity is only tenuously confined within a physical body. We are concerned because the person in question is so poor that he barely has enough to eat. If I promise to bear in mind a request you make, this does not mean that it will be filed away in a mysterious way in an ethereal filing cabinet in, but not physically in, a ghostly place called my mind. You would be dissatisfied if that were all that I did mean by it, for you would quite rightly understand my promise as a commitment on my part seriously to consider what you have asked me with a view to acting upon it. Similarly to say that someone's heart is in the right place is not normally taken to be an observation about his anatomical structure.

In none of these cases do we misunderstand what is said because it has been expressed in a way which "literally", as one might put it, means something else. There is often a difference between a particular meaning which is implied or suggested by a form of words, and the point which someone is trying to make by the use of that expression. Failure to appreciate this has led to some unnecessarily contentious disputes in philosophy. An example is the lengthy and confused disagreement which took place over the issue of the existence or non-existence of propositions. Let us take it that a proposition is the meaning of a sentence. Then, a way of saying that sentences have meanings is to say that propositions exist. But some people object to this statement, because the form of words seems to imply that there are entities called propositions existing somewhere in the universe. In that case, they argue, the statement is absurd since no sense can be given to the notion of the existence or non-existence of such entities. We should have no idea how to recognise a proposition if we came across one, for it is not the sort of thing which can be detected by sense-perception. So, to deny the absurdity of this implication they deny that propositions exist. At this their opponents can point out that their very denial is self-defeating, for the form of words used in the denial, since it can unquestionably be understood, must itself have meaning—which implies that at least one proposition exists.

A more obvious example of words being understood in a non-literal way is that of a tennis player trying to eradicate certain faults in his service action. After a considerable period of determined practice he reaches an exasperating stage of helplessness where, so far from improving his service, his efforts seem to have made it far worse. At this point an experienced and perceptive coach, accurately diagnosing his difficulty, might advise him to stop trying. Such advice is often beneficial in the teaching of a variety of activities, but of course, despite the form of words he uses, the coach does not for a moment intend his pupil to abandon the attempt to improve his service. On the contrary, his object is to reduce the inhibiting tension induced by the determination to succeed. And it is by no means an uncommon experience that such advice has the desired effect of helping the pupil to relax and produce a more effective, more appropriately directed effort. This is the point of the advice to stop trying, and the pupil would certainly understand it in this way. The coach would be surprised if his pupil, on being told to stop trying, put down his racket and walked off the court to sit on a bench.

As long as we are aware of the point of what is said it does not usually matter that it is expressed in a form of words which could be understood in a different way. Thus it is not necessarily unintelligible to talk in a way which appears to accept the traditional view. We can distinguish between a dance which "springs from the soul" and one which doesn't.

The difference is there to be seen in the performances themselves, if we are sufficiently discerning to appreciate it.

The danger of serious confusion and error arises only when we take too literally the picture of the inaccessible inner mind, soul, spirit, or emotion as the source of expressive meaning. For, in the aesthetic sphere, this leads to the gravely mistaken notion that reasoned discussion about interpretation of dance and the arts generally, is entirely inappropriate. And this pervasive misconception has for too long distorted or truncated an important aspect of involvement with the arts. It certainly is true that one often reaches a position of irreconcilable disagreement about aesthetic merit or meaning, but at least equally often one does engage in an illuminating exchange of conflicting views, and with a genuine possibility of reaching at least a measure of agreement. Unless one is hopelessly bigoted one can change one's mind about a painting, a play, a piece of music or a dance, as a result of listening with an open mind to someone else's perceptive reasoning. We shall examine more fully later what is involved in giving a rational justification of an aesthetic judgment. At this stage of the argument it is enough simply to cite our common experience of adducing reasons for the way we see the arts. We go to a cinema, a theatre, a concert, an art gallery, and frequently have such widely differing interpretations that it promotes lively and enlightening discussion. In aesthetic appreciation, no less than in other spheres, those who will never genuinely listen to differing views live impoverished lives.

The danger of confusion which leads to a denial of the possibility of giving reasons for one's response to art arises from our tendency to take too literally a picture which impregnates our language. If, when it is said that a particular movement springs from the inner feeling of the dancer, this is taken as a reference to the sincerity and intensity of the performance, revealed in observable features of the dance itself, then no confusion need arise. But only too often such a statement leads to the notion that in that case the meaning of expressive movement can be understood only by achieving some mysterious communication with a normally inaccessible mental entity in order to establish its relation with the outer physical movements.

The decisive movement in the conjuring trick which leads us to accept this incoherent notion, is the pervasive belief that the meaning of a word is an object, in this case an inner feeling. To think in this way is to make the same sort of mistake as those who feel that they have to deny that propositions exist, since no one has ever seen a proposition, as one can see mountains and giraffes. It is to make the same sort of mistake as the tennis pupil who walks off the court when he is told to stop trying.

Wittgenstein (1953 § 308) on the analogous case of remembering:

> The impression that we wanted to deny something arises from our setting our faces against the picture of the "inner process". What we deny is that the picture of the inner process gives us the correct idea of the use of the word "to remember". We say that this picture with its ramifications stands in the way of our seeing the use of the word as it is.
>
> Why should I deny that there is a mental process? But "There has just taken place in me the mental process of remembering . . ." means nothing more than: "I have just remembered . . ." To deny the mental process would mean to deny the remembering; to deny that anyone ever remembers anything."

The main import of the argument so far is to expose the seminal and pernicious error inherent in the traditional view, which would have it that mind and body, expression and movement are two separate *things*. Yet this is not to deny the facts which often lead us to say, for example, that a certain student has a quick and incisive mind. Neither is it to deny that there is a significant difference between a dancer who is merely technically accomplished, and a dancer whose movements are both technically accomplished and also sensitively expressive. There are various ways in which people express in words the difference between two such performances. Some of these verbal expressions have a much greater tendency to mislead than others, and for that reason it may be wiser to eschew those which suggest the picture of the spirit within. Nevertheless, expressions like "Her movements spring from her inner feeling" are not necessarily meaningless or misleading. They can be quite unexceptionable as long as it is clear that they are drawing attention to observable features of the movements themselves.

In short, we do not have two *things*, a body and a mind, or a physical movement and an emotion. It is less misleading to say that we have one thing, a body, which we use in various ways, some of which are intellectual or mental. And we have one thing, a physical movement, but we can perform it in an emotionally expressive way.

It may be helpful at this point to summarise the position. It has been shown to be unintelligible to regard the meaning of an expressive movement as given by a necessarily private, inner activity called an emotion. To understand the plausibility of this view we exposed three tenacious fallacies about meaning in language. We saw that:

(1) The meaning of a word is not isolated and rigidly fixed. It can be understood only in the context of the living language of which it is a constituent part.

(2) Naming is not the only nor even the primary function of words in language.

(3) The meaning of a word is not an object.

It is important to be clear about linguistic meaning not only because we are discussing in words the notion of expression in movement, but also because it is illuminating to compare the meaning of words in language with the meaning of expressive movements, in both aesthetic and non-aesthetic contexts.

C:

BEHAVIOURISM

(1) Scientific explanation of actions

There is a danger that the foregoing argument to show the incoherence of traditional dualism may be understood as lending support to an equally mistaken though common theory which I shall call behaviourism. The particular theory I shall discuss is not the only version of behaviourism, but most, if not all, versions share the same major underlying assumptions. Moreover, many people, especially among those with scientific, psychological and sociological training, implicitly retain these assumptions while explicitly denying that they are behaviourists. This may be because the term "behaviourism" is often associated with certain theories which have been rejected or modified on *scientific* grounds, while the *conceptual* fallacies inherent in those views are frequently taken over uncritically. These are the fallacies which we need to examine, for they are more fundamental, and more seriously misleading.

Behaviourism is the belief that every aspect of human action is in principle explicable in exclusively causal or scientific terms. Perhaps it can most clearly be understood by tracing out how this conclusion is reached.

The behaviourist is well aware that the notion of a non-physical inner emotion which has some sort of unverifiable causal connection with physical movements is unintelligible. No sense can be made of a causal relationship between two events which the traditional theory itself insists are so logically dissimilar. We have seen that the emotional or aesthetic meaning of an expressive movement can be understood only by paying attention to the movement itself. This seems to imply that an interest in expressive movement is an interest in a purely physical phenomenon. In general it seems to imply that talk of mental activities and attributes makes sense only when understood as obliquely referring to physical phenomena, and since anything physical can be examined scientifically it is taken to follow that mental characteristics, to be intelligible, must be examinable in the same way. For example, if it is said that someone is an intelligent hockey player, this is to be understood not as referring to the activity of a mythical mental entity, but as an indication of the way in which he performs physical movements on the hockey field. Since all such movements can be examined scientifically the behaviourist takes it that intelligence, and all other mental characteristics, can be examined scientifically.

Behaviourism, then, is a form of reductionism, in that mental statements, including emotion statements, are reduced to statements about behaviour, which is taken to be comprehensively explicable, in principle, in scientific terms. It is usually suggested not that all behaviour can at present be explained in this way, but that it is merely a matter of time before scientific knowledge has advanced to that point.

There is a sense in which it is unexceptionable to say that mental statements can be understood only by reference to physical behaviour, but in the sense understood by the behaviourist it is a serious misconception whose plausibility depends upon one or both of the following very natural, if mistaken, assumptions:

(a) that action or behaviour can be intelligibly explained only in causal, physical, scientific terms.

(b) that the notion of the unique position of the agent with respect to his mental experience has been exploded as a myth along with the traditional view of inner, mental states.

Inextricably bound up with the former is the belief that men cannot have free will, for, it is argued, if every human action is causally determined, and therefore predictable, we cannot be free to choose what we do. But the assumption that behaviour is purely a matter of physical and chemical interaction is profoundly mistaken, as can be illustrated by adapting an analogy used by Ryle (1949).

Suppose that someone with scientific training, but no knowledge of games, is invited to try to work out for himself, by observation, what is involved in playing tennis. For simplicity the experiment is restricted to a game of singles. After watching for a while he begins to appreciate that there are rules which limit the players' freedom of action in certain ways. They must keep the ball within the singles court, they must serve into a particular area, they must not allow the ball to bounce more than once, they must change sides after each rally in order to deliver and receive service respectively etc. The longer the observer watches, the more of these rules he discovers. Now if he were imbued with a misconception about the nature of explanation similar to that of the behaviourist, he might come to a conclusion something like this:

"What a boring activity tennis must be. The players have no choice since the area to which they are allowed to play each ball is already specified in advance. They cannot even serve twice consecutively into the same service court if they so wish. Everything they do is governed by the rules of the game. It is true that I have not yet discovered the laws which prescribe the exact part of the court to which each respective shot must be hit in order to count as legitimate, but this is merely a matter of time. After all, I thought at first that the players could choose the side from which to serve, and that they could have as many attempts at serving as they wished, but now I find that a player is allowed a maximum of two attempts, and that after each rally he has to change sides for his next service. Further observation will reveal all the other rules, and it will then be possible for me to predict, at every juncture of the game, how and to which precise section of the court the ball must be hit. The game is so rigidly restricted that there is no scope for freedom and initiative."

It is perfectly true that further observation may reveal more rules, for example, it may be some time before he becomes aware of those which are infrequently invoked, such as the prohibition on a double hit, and on striking the net during a rally. But to argue from his increasing understanding of the rules to the conclusion that he will eventually be able to predict precisely how and where each ball has to be played, is a fallacy. He will search in vain for the *rule* which determines why, at a particular stage of the game, a player hoists a lob over his opponent's head instead of trying to produce a backhand passing shot, as he has done previously when in this position. The observer's mistake is to assume that tennis can be explained only in terms of the rules, and that since rules cover every stroke played there can be no freedom to exercise the individual initiative which alone would make the game interesting. Yet, on the contrary, to have no rules would make the game boring by eliminating the possibility of intelligent, imaginative play. Tactical skill can operate only within a framework. If this is not immediately obvious, just think what would happen if all the rules of tennis were removed, so that one could hit the ball anywhere and anyhow. How, in this situation could there be any scope for intelligent tactical manoeuvre? The observer's preconception does not allow him to appreciate that there are at least two ways of explaining each shot, one legal and one tactical. Suppose, for example, one of the players were asked "Why did you hit the ball there?" He could reply either in terms of the rules, e.g. "Well, if I had hit it any deeper it would have been out of court, and I should have lost the point," or in terms of tactics, e.g. "I realised that my opponent was particularly susceptible to deep shots into the backhand court." The logical character of each explanation is quite different, and therefore there is no conflict between them.

Similarly, since every human action is governed by laws of physical causation, the behaviourist concludes that there can be no freedom. But to assume that human behaviour can be explained only by scientific laws is to ignore reasons for choosing to behave in certain ways. It is like assuming that tennis can be explained only by the rules. The behaviourist has failed to understand that the logical character of causes is quite different from the logical character of reasons, and therefore there can be no conflict between them and neither of them can exclude the other. Just as the rules of a game do not preclude choice of tactics, so causal determination of actions does not preclude free will. Because he has been trained to look for causes, the behaviourist is usually unaware that his notion of explanation is limited, indeed, he tends to be convinced that he is entirely open-minded. He may say, for instance, "I am quite ready to accept any claim for which sound evidence can be produced." Yet to restrict justification to scientific evidence is itself limiting. To put the point paradoxically, it is to be open-minded, but only within limits.

This implicit restriction of explanation to one logical type is like taking strict adherence to the formal structure as the only important feature of a sonnet. A sonnet has to be fourteen lines in length, written in iambic pentameters with a particular rhyming scheme. Yet stringent conformity to these requirements is not the only, nor even the most important, aspect to be considered. To say that a sonnet is written strictly in accordance with the formal requirements is to say little, if anything, about its aesthetic merit. It may be that I can write sonnets which are structurally as correct as any written by Shakespeare. Indeed, I can do better, for he is sometimes a little wayward in this respect, but that does not imply that mine are as good as or even better than his. The misconception of assuming that human behaviour is a purely causal matter is like taking the formal structure as the only criterion of merit in a sonnet. And the behaviourist's consequent insistence that causal determination precludes freedom is like assuming that the rigidity of the sonnet form precludes freedom of poetic expression. Yet so far from being artistically crippling, the formal stringency is the very feature which allows a sonnet-writer of Shakespeare's calibre to manifest poetic merit. In the same way J. S. Bach's supreme artistry in composition was revealed not despite but because of the restrictions imposed by the fugal form, among others.

The behaviourist's assumption that only scientific explanations are legitimate leads to, or is part of, the belief that ultimate reality is a matter of what can be weighed, measured and empirically tested. It is sometimes said, for example, that only scientists discover what really exists, the rest of us are mere amateurs indulging in vague speculation. (Notice again the use of that fishy word "really".) This view is put forward in various ways which claim or imply that scientific procedures are more factual, more objective, more definite, more reliable etc. than other methods of discovery.

One certainly would not wish to deny or minimise the value of scientific explanations. But just as definitions, in the strict sense of logical equivalence, are useful for explaining the meanings of some words, yet misleading when applied to others, so causal, scientific explanations are valuable only if we are aware of the sphere in which they are appropriate. Take, for example, the claim that the only or the ultimate reality about a painting is what can be scientifically assessed. A chemist and a physicist may be able to determine precisely the material constitution of the paint, canvas and frame, and this might well yield interesting and valuable information. Yet, a comprehensive list of the physical properties of a painting tells us nothing whatsoever about its aesthetic quality, and the aesthetic quality is just as real as its physical properties. The behaviourist fails to appreciate that there is a way of looking at a painting other than in terms of its chemical and physical composition.[1]

There is a sense in which aesthetic quality depends upon

---

[1] For a discussion of this issue in relation specifically to dance see Best (1973).

material composition. If a painter could not rely upon his materials, he could not be subtle and precise in his work. It would be a matter of chance, and that is to say that the art of painting as we know it could not exist. Similarly the expressive character of a movement depends upon causal and mechanical factors, for if there were a failure of interaction between bones, joints and muscles there could be no expression in movement. Furthermore, as can be seen particularly clearly in the case of op. art, scientific discoveries sometimes actually alter the possibility of artistic expression by providing different materials and apparatus. In the same way, changing the rules of a game changes the tactical possibilities—examples are the experiment with a new off-side law in soccer, the tie-breaker in tennis and the change in the law of leg before wicket in cricket. And the exercise-physiologist may be able to suggest ways in which a dancer could improve her technique. But it is important to recognise, in each of these cases, the different logical status of the respective factors. Though one factor may set limits to the other, neither is reducible to the other. The improved physical proficiency in the dancer's movements is not the same thing as, nor does it necessarily confer, improved aesthetic quality. It may allow for a more extensive range of expressive movement, through greater control and dexterity, for example, yet what is expressed in that movement is not a matter for scientific assessment.

A similar failure to recognise the limits of causal explanation is prevalent among some educational and sociological theorists. Good evidence is produced that adverse environmental conditions, at home and at school, have a detrimental effect on children's academic attainment. Academic differences are then taken to be uniquely attributable to the fact that some children live and work in poor conditions, others in healthier, more congenial conditions. Therefore, it is believed, as we improve the physical conditions of those who are now deprived, we shall progressively move towards a position of academic equality.

Those who reach this conclusion are no doubt already

predisposed towards it because they are in the grip of certain political, sociological or educational theories. But the argument is confused. It takes a valid point to an invalid extreme. Causal influences, though important are not the only factors relevant to academic, or indeed other human attainments. It may well be true that deprived children could not improve their standards in school work without an improvement in their environmental conditions, for physical conditions set limits to intellectual capability just as they do to artistic expression. But that is not to say that equally good physical conditions will necessarily lead to equally good academic levels, for reasons, as well as causes, have to be taken into account. For example motivation, an appeal to the intentions of children, is also an important factor, and that is on a different logical level from causal, physical factors. In short, it is one thing to hold that there are causally necessary conditions for high educational attainment, quite another to hold that there are causally sufficient conditions, or that such attainment is constituted by environmental factors.

Furthermore, there are variations in natural aptitude for intellectual as well as for sporting activities. A tennis coach giving a group of beginners the same teaching and facilities would not expect to produce a number of equally good players. Some, for instance, would have a better "eye for a ball" than others.

The behaviourist is unable to appreciate that there may be more than one way to answer a question. This is partly because the sort of answer required is usually so obvious from the circumstances in which the question is asked that it is easy to assume there is no other way to reply. Consider the following examples of how the context may determine the sort of answer required.

One evening I go to watch a match at the local cricket club, and I notice, on arriving, that one of the opening batsmen, who is known for his cautious if reliable play, is still batting. Suddenly, to my astonishment, he leaps down the wicket, swings wildly at a good delivery from the bowler, completely misses the ball and is comprehensively bowled.

"Why did he do that?" I ask. It is obvious from the context that my question is a request for a reason for a surprisingly uncharacteristic, and apparently foolhardy action. The answer is "Because that was the last ball of the match and his team needed five runs to win. His only hope of winning was to take a chance and try to hit a six." So, though normally cautious, he had to take a risk on this occasion.

For those who do not understand cricket, the example can be translated into basketball terms.[1] An American friend is explaining to me the functions of the various team members as we watch a game. He tells me, among other details, that the normal rôle of the play-maker is to create openings for other players to score baskets. He does not often attempt to shoot, especially since he usually operates at some distance from the basket. After we have been watching for some time, the play-maker suddenly takes what seems to me an absurdly wild shot when he is so far away from the basket that he has very little hope of success. "Why did he do that?" I ask. "Because his team is one point down and the final buzzer is about to sound. His only hope of winning the contest is to take a desperation last-second shot." Again, it is clear from the circumstances in which I ask the question that it is a request for a reason for the unusual action of the play-maker.

But a different context may create quite different expectations about the sort of explanation which is appropriate. Suppose that a group of scientists are trying to discover whether certain bio-mechanical and psychological factors affect the ability to play games. At present they are examining cricketers and basketball players, and they have already reached certain tentative conclusions. The question, "Why did he do that?" asked of the batsman or the play-maker, in *this* context, is likely to be answered very differently, for it would amount to a request for a causal, scientific explanation. So, though the question might seem to allow for only one sort of intelligible reply, in fact there can

[1] I am indebted to Dr. Richard Terry, of Castleton State College, Vermont, for suggesting and clarifying the details of this example.

be an explanation in terms of reasons, e.g. "The team needed five runs to win," or in terms of causes, e.g. "He has quick reflexes and strong forearms." To assume, as the behaviourist does, that only a causal explanation makes sense, is a fundamental misconception.

This dual possibility in answering a question is sometimes used to advantage in jokes or evasions. "Why have you come home drunk on our wedding anniversary?" asks the irate wife. "Because I drank a large quantity of beer before leaving the pub." This sort of answer is more likely to exacerbate than to mollify the indignation of the wife, who is well enough aware of, and not at present interested in, the *cause* of her husband's drunkenness. What she wants to know is the *reason* for it.

These examples are introduced to show that reasons cannot be reduced to causes, even though both types of explanation may be given of every intentional action. Although it makes no sense to regard a statement about mental or emotional characteristics as answerable to inaccessible inner events, it does not follow that it is intelligible only as an oblique reference to purely physical phenomena which are in principle open to scientific examination. The underlying error of the behaviourist is a failure to understand the logical status of minds. He cannot distinguish between:

(a) There are such things as minds
and
(b) There are such *things* as minds.

So he either dismisses minds as metaphysical nonsense, or insists that they stand up to scientific examination like every other *thing*. That is, he is suspicious that one is indulging in fairy stories since there is no evidence of minds, unless "mind" is another way of referring to something physical like the brain, for which there *is* evidence. He is in a position similar to that of those philosophers who want to deny that propositions exist since no empirical evidence can be produced for them. This is rather like refusing to accept that the average family has 2.4 children on the grounds that it is impossible for any family to have 2.4 children. To deny that there are minds unless evidence can be produced for their existence betrays the same sort of.confusion, for to say that people have minds is not like saying they have heads. Heads can be measured empirically, but minds cannot be measured in this way.

To say that people have minds is a shorthand to refer to the fact that they have a great variety of mental and emotional experiences and characteristics. Thus it is unlikely that the behaviourist is denying what *we* mean by saying that people have minds, for that would amount to a refusal to accept such obvious facts as these, which is a quite untenable position. If, on the other hand, the behaviourist who denies that people have minds means that there is nothing which can be empirically identified as a mind, in the way in which one can identify a head, then there is no disagreement between us. Once the distinction is clearly understood, the disagreement dissolves, for in saying that people have minds we are making no such claim as that they have, physically in their possession, spatially locatable, empirically measurable objects called minds. We are saying, *inter alia,* that people think, are happy and sad, feel pain.

Specifically, the expressive meaning of an action, though a characteristic of the movement itself, cannot be explained in purely anatomical, physiological or other scientific terms. For it is simply not that sort of characteristic, any more than the average citizen is the sort of person to whom you can introduce me.

C:

BEHAVIOURISM

(2) The mental experience

The second misconception of behaviourism is to assume that the notion of the peculiar position of the agent, the person who has the mental experience, is discredited as part of the traditional view. This, though a very understandable oversight, is to throw out the baby with the bathwater. It is to fail to take account of what Wisdom calls the asymmetrical logic of psychological questions.

Having rejected the possibility of explaining human actions by reference to unobservable inner events, the behaviourist concentrates with inappropriate exclusiveness on the observable outer events. He insists that there is no way of knowing anything about the mental and emotional other than by perceiving the physical. He overlooks the fact that, though we can find out about someone's feelings only by watching his behaviour, that person himself does not discover by observation that he is feeling something. It is true that sometimes other people more accurately diagnose the character of my emotion than I do myself, and it is also true that it would be impossible to understand my own feelings if it were not possible in general to know what others are feeling. But this is not to say that I can discover that I am feeling an emotion only by observing my own actions.

Wisdom (1952):

> The peculiarity of the soul is not that it is visible to none but that it is visible to one.

This is not intended to support the unintelligible notion of an inner mind or soul, but as a reminder that, though the traditional view is mistaken, it nevertheless incorporates an element of truth which the behaviourist has missed. In his eagerness to repudiate the traditionalist's metaphysical entities, the behaviourist tends to forget, or even to deny, that the person who is experiencing an emotion is in a different position for knowing about it from anyone else. For it is certainly not necessary for me to observe my own behaviour, or to consult other people who have been watching my behaviour, in order to know *that* I am feeling an emotion even if I am mistaken about *what* emotion it is. This point is even more obvious in the case of sensations. We can tell from our observation of his groans and writhing that a road-accident victim is in severe pain, but he does not need to observe his behaviour in order to know that he is in pain. He simply *has* the pain, and he is only too well aware of it without self-examination or asking anyone else about his behaviour. This is what Wisdom means by the asymmetrical logic of psychological statements—the position of the person experiencing a sensation or emotion is not symmetrical with that of anyone else. Others, unlike the agent himself, can learn of his mental state only by means of his behaviour, including his verbal behaviour.

Notice how this turn in the argument appears to put us in danger of slipping back towards a belief in inner mental events. Philosophical mistakes are not stupid mistakes. There is a point of substance in the traditionalist's recognition of the two ways of knowing about mental experiences, even though he is mistaken about the relation between them. He is right to insist that I have a way of knowing that I am in pain which no one else has, but he is wrong to assume from this that consequently only I can really know that I am in pain, only I can be certain, whereas other people can have only indirect knowledge via the evidence of my bodily actions.

On the other hand, the behaviourist is right to insist that others can really know that I am in pain simply by observing my behaviour. But he is wrong to assume from this that consequently the only way of knowing that pain is being felt is by observing behaviour.

This asymmetry creates another fatal objection to the behaviourist's belief that mental statements can be reduced to behaviour statements. He agrees with the traditionalist that, where other people are concerned, the only evidence which is available to support conclusions about mental characteristics and events is behavioural evidence. Yet he also points out the unintelligibility of the proposed move from premises about observable behaviour to conclusions about inaccessible mental events, that is, from premises of one logical type to conclusions of a completely different logical type. The behaviourist recognises that there is nothing other than behaviour which can allow us to draw conclusions about the minds of others. He draws attention to the fact that, unlike minds, physical bodies can be seen, weighed and measured. And, since there is no evidence of anything other than physical behaviour, he argues, plausibly enough, that statements about minds, if they are to make sense at all, simply *are* statements about behavioural evidence, that their meanings are identical.

But there is no logical implication either way between "John is writhing and groaning," and "John is in pain," in the sense that it would be self-contradictory to assert one while denying the other. It may be that John is pretending to be in pain, or, conversely, he may be in pain without revealing it. We have already seen that it is as impossible generally to be mistaken about the emotions of others as it is for most people most of the time to tell lies, but that is not to say that one cannot on occasions be mistaken about the character of expressive movement and pain behaviour of others, or that one cannot be deceived by lies. So "John is writhing and groaning" cannot simply *mean* "John is in pain," since John can be writhing and groaning without being in pain.

To see how natural it is for the behaviourist to fall into this error, consider the case of a scientist who is trying to discover whether there is a relation between emotional states and level of blood-pressure. He carries out a large number of tests on a large number of people, and observes that whenever someone is sad his blood pressure goes down. He concludes that there is a correlation between sadness and low blood-pressure. Another way of putting this would be to say that low blood pressure means sadness. And this formulation seems to lend support to the behaviourist's contention that emotions can be identified with physical evidence, for there is a sense in which it is unexceptionable to claim, in this case, that low blood pressure means sadness. But that sense will not provide the relationship the behaviourist requires for his argument to go through. The ambiguity of the verb "to mean" tends to obscure an important distinction here—there are at least two senses:

(a) A means B = A is a sign of B, e.g. heavy oil consumption means a worn engine.

(b) A means B = A is logically equivalent to or logically implies B, e.g. "bachelor" means "unmarried man."

There may be conclusive empirical evidence that low blood pressure is a sign of sadness, but the behaviourist is mistaken to assume that therefore low blood pressure logically implies or is identical with sadness. On the contrary, the connection between them is contingent, and had to be established by scientific experiment. It is like discovering by observation that there is a connection between turning windmill sails and a wind blowing. In this case too, if I see the sails turning I should be entitled to say "That means there is a wind blowing," but clearly this is to use "means" in sense (a). The turning sails are a sign of the wind. It certainly does not follow logically from the meaning of "The sails are turning" that there is a wind blowing. It would not be self-contradictory to say "The sails are turning but there is no wind"—perhaps a mechanical device has been installed, for instance. Yet it would be self-contradictory to speak of a bachelor who is not an unmarried man. It happens to be the case that there is a connection between wind and turning sails, and between low blood pressure and sadness. We arrive at these conclusions by observations, experiment, evidence, but the connection between a bachelor and an unmarried man is not of this sort. We do not need to carry out surveys and experiments to discover that bachelors are unmarried men. Perhaps there are windmills whose sails turn in the absence of wind, and people whose blood pressure remains normal when they are sad, but what sense could we make of the suggestion that perhaps we might one day discover a bachelor who is married? The impossibility in this case is logical, it is a matter of the meanings of words.

Thus there is no logical connection, still less identity of meaning, between low blood pressure and sadness. The scientist cannot discover the evidence for sadness *independently* of knowing what it is for people to be sad. Or, to put the point another way, he has to have a way of knowing that people are sad *before* he can attempt to establish the correlation with low blood pressure. The very use of the term "correlation" gives the game away, for it can be legitimately employed only with respect to two separately identifiable phenomena. The evidence for sadness cannot be the same as the sadness itself.

If there is a question about the level of someone's blood pressure, or about the size, shape and colour of material objects, then it is a contingent matter if some people are in a better position to answer it than others. But if the question is "Does Barbara feel sad?" then Barbara has a way of knowing the answer which is not available to anyone else, and which is not contingently alterable. We can all, in principle anyway, go and check the blood pressure, whereas we cannot all go and feel the sadness. There is an asymmetry of position for verification which defeats the behaviourist's contention that statements about minds can be reduced to statements about behavioural or other physical evidence.

There is a danger of misunderstanding what is involved in this asymmetry. It might be thought that a statement such as "John is in pain" must have two meanings, one meaning is given by his external behaviour and is understood by observers, the other is given by the feeling of pain and is understood only by John. So, for every psychological statement there seems to be both an objective and a subjective meaning. Yet this would lead us right back to the problems confronting the traditional view, since there would be no way of knowing whether there is any relation between the two meanings. Our judgement, as spectators, that John is in pain, on the basis of his behaviour, would have no connection with what John is feeling. So that, though we have seen him accidentally hit his thumb with a hammer, and he now curses, screws up his face and wrings his hand, for all we know, as spectators, he might be enjoying pleasurable sensations.

There is no need to accept that there are two meanings simply on account of the difference of position for knowing the truth of what is said. It often happens, in contexts other than that of mental experience, that people are in different positions for verifying a statement about whose single meaning they are all agreed. Consider the following hypothetical case.

Peter Laradiddle is a popular British tennis player in local tournaments. This year, to everyone's surprise, he just managed to scrape through the qualifying rounds of the Wimbledon tennis tournament. He is drawn against the number one seed in the men's singles. Naturally enough he is given no chance at all of winning the match. However, at some time during the afternoon there is a rumour, "Peter Laradiddle has won the first two sets." This arouses excited incredulity, and those who hear it are eager to know whether it is true. But, though there are various methods which are appropriate for verifying it, the people who hear the rumour all take it to mean the same thing. Someone who has a good seat on Centre Court, but who is napping in the sun, has only to open his eyes and look at the score. Someone who is elsewhere on the ground can walk to Centre Court and see for himself. Someone working in the centre of London might telephone the Club. Someone in California might rush to turn on the radio or television, hoping for a newsflash, and there are many more possibilities. Despite the fact that there are various verification procedures, there is only one meaning. Only by adopting an inappropriate procedure might one show that one had understood the rumour to mean something different. For example, if someone telephoned the national hair styles competition to ask whether Peter Laradiddle had won the first two classes in ladies hair sets, that would show that he had misunderstood the rumour, and taken it to mean something different. So, as long as they are appropriate, the fact that there are various ways of checking the truth of a statement does not show that it has several meanings. Similarly, though there are two different ways of knowing whether Barbara is sad, depending on whether or not one is Barbara, this does not imply that the statement "Barbara is sad," has two meanings.

The Wimbledon example was given to illustrate that the meaning of a statement does not change simply because there are different ways of verifying it, and this is equally true of a statement about mental experience. However, this should not be allowed to blur the significant difference between the two cases which has just been pointed out, for whereas we can all, in principle anyway, go to Centre Court to check the score directly, we cannot all feel the mental experience. It may be contingently the case that several people are in different positions for finding out whether Barbara is sad, just as they are for ascertaining the tennis score, but for mental experiences it is always the case that one person is in a position which no one else could possibly be in. Others have to depend upon her behaviour, including her verbal behaviour, in order to find out that Barbara is sad, but only Barbara simply has the feeling of sadness.

D:

BODY/MIND
THEORIES COMPARED

(1) Behaviourism, solipsism,
and the traditional theory

In order to bring out the salient points of the problem concerning the logical status of a mind, and its relationship with the body, we shall now go on to contrast behaviourism with its polar opposite, as well as with the, in some respects, intermediate traditional view. An understanding of the relative strengths of these three theories will reveal those features which are necessary to any adequate solution of the problem.

Though behaviourism fails to take account of the psychological experience itself, this is by no means a careless or stupid oversight. This is why it is necessary to see not only that the theory is mistaken but also how it is that people are led to believe it, otherwise there is a danger of losing sight of the genuine features it is stressing, though to the point of inappropriate over-emphasis. In fact, the behaviourist does not usually make the oversimple claim that groaning just *is* pain. More typically he would say that the statement that someone is in pain is equivalent to a more complex set of statements about his bodily state and physical actions. What more can one do, asks the behaviourist, to discover whether someone is in pain than to watch his behaviour and his facial expression, to carry out a medical examination of his body for cuts, bruises, swellings etc.? One depends solely upon what can be publicly perceived.

But this way of arguing puts the behaviourist in an embarrassing position. External behaviour may be the only data available, yet inevitably it comes to us through our senses. Even though the scientist does his best to be precise and to eliminate the possibility of human error, by employing highly sophisticated instruments when he conducts his laboratory experiments, in the end he still depends upon the deliverances of human faculties. A microscope enlarges and sharpens the possibility of seeing, but not for a blind man. A stethoscope, or an amplifier, gives greater scope for hearing, but not to a deaf man. So we can ascertain the mental states of others only through our own powers of perception. Indeed, to generalise the point, all knowledge must come through our own sense perception. Thus, so far from the external, objective and empirically measurable being the ultimate reality, as is claimed by the behaviourist, it begins to look as though the internal, subjective and immeasurably mysterious entity which receives the mental experiences is that ultimate reality.

Wittgenstein (1962, 5.62) once wrote:

> What solipsism *means* is quite correct.

Solipsism is the theory that the self is the only knowable or existent thing. That is, not only am I the only one who can know of my own experiences, but also my experiences are all that can be known. The theory can best be understood, perhaps, as the polar opposite to behaviourism. Realising the incoherence of the traditionalist's inference from outer bodily action to inner mental events, the behaviourist believes that all is outer, while the solipsist believes that all is inner, i.e. that each of us is immutably locked into his own private mental prison, with no possibility of ever coming to know anything outside it. Indeed, for the solipsist, the very notion of anything outside it makes no sense. As Wittgenstein put it, the world is *my* world (1962; 5.62).

It would take us too far afield adequately to discuss this theory, and anyway it does not appeal to many people, since it insists that nothing exists other than one's own mind, but it is relevant to our interests to see the strength of the case for it. In the remarks quoted above, Wittgenstein was not implying that he supported solipsism, but was drawing attention to an important element of truth in it, which is overlooked by behaviourism.

Jonathan Bennett (1966) puts the point this way:

> A problem exists for me only if I have it; evidence which solves the problem exists for me only if I have it. Someone else may have evidence which bears upon my problem, but I cannot take such evidence into account until I have it too. And when someone tells me what he knows about something, he provides me with new evidence only by confronting me with new sensory data.

And later;

> My Weltanschauung and my conceptual scheme must ultimately rest upon my experience, including my intake of the reports of others on their experience.

It may be difficult to accept that nothing exists except one's own mind, that the world is my world, yet there is undeniably something in the contention that everything that can be known has to come through the media of sense-impressions. The solipsist may have taken his argument to an extreme, but only as a result of his clear recognition of two valid points:

(a) that the causal inference from observable outer behaviour to unobservable inner mental events, on which the traditional view depends, is incoherent.

(b) that experience is always *somebody's* experience.

The behaviourist agrees about the former point but seems to forget the latter. He is so insistent that observable behaviour is the only way of knowing about mental experience that he overlooks the fact that someone is *having* the experience. Nevertheless, his reaching that position reveals a clear recognition of two valid points:

(a) that the causal inference of the traditionalist is incoherent.
(b) that we come to know about the mental states of others only by observing their behaviour.

The traditional theorist rejects solipsism because of its conclusion that one can never know anything outside oneself. He points out that of course we can learn of the experiences of others. Most of us, for example, have not climbed on Everest, yet it is of considerable interest to hear what happened to Don Whillans on that mountain. Thus we are not limited to our own experiences. In this the traditionalist agrees with the behaviourist, but he disagrees with the latter's stress on observable physical evidence to the exclusion of the experience itself. For to ignore what the agent feels or to imagine that he knows about his feeling by means of behavioural evidence, is to make a fundamental mistake. In· this the traditionalist is of the same opinion as the solipsist. So the traditional theory consists of one valid point taken from, and mistakenly exaggerated by, each of the other theories. These are:

(a) that experience is always somebody's experience, and the person concerned does not have to discover its occurrence by observation.
(b) that it is solely by means of their observable behaviour that we learn of the experiences of others.

Thus the traditionalist concludes that one has direct

knowledge of one's own mind, but only indirect knowledge of others' minds. However, we found that talk of direct and indirect knowledge makes no sense in this sphere. It makes sense to speak of finding out indirectly that there is a wind by watching windmill sails turning, and directly by going out and feeling it blowing in our faces. But it is impossible to get inside someone's mind to find out directly what his external behaviour is expressing. So though we can agree that traditional dualism has correctly located the genuine insights of solipsism and behaviourism, it is clear that the proposed connection between them is unintelligible. Nevertheless, it is perfectly true that any coherent theory of mind must be adequate *both* to personal experience *and* to physical behaviour. Specifically, it must coherently explain the relation between expressive bodily movement and the emotion it is expressing.

D:

BODY/MIND
THEORIES COMPARED

(2) Mysticism

Any satisfactory theory of the relationship between mental experiences and physical behaviour has, then, to take account of the genuine insights expressed in each of the theories we have considered, while rejecting the fallacies contained in them. And since the traditional theory incorporates the valid aspects of the solipsist's and behaviourist's stress on mind and body respectively, but goes wrong over the connection between them, it would seem profitable to look more carefully at the sort of connection which would be adequate.

The relation between bodily actions and mental events certainly cannot be merely contingent or fortuitous, one which just happens to be the case. It cannot just happen to be the case that the writhing and groaning of the road accident victim correlates with his feeling of pain. There will somehow have to be a guarantee that, at least for the most part, certain sorts of physical behaviour necessarily relate to certain sorts of mental experience.

One frequently encountered type of theory which we mentioned briefly in section B (4), and which appreciates this necessity can be broadly termed mysticism or transcendentalism, i.e. a belief that ultimately the mental or spiritual meaning of all physical actions is given by reference to a deity, or to cosmic laws, by a spiritual apprehension of truths beyond normal understanding. Thus, as a general example, Meerloo (1962) says:

> Many mystics speak of the sacred depersonalization and holy union with the universe. The very word "ecstasy" expresses this reaching out beyond man's limitations...as a magic surrender to a different existence, as a transcendence of oneself. Lost in rhythm man can forget his worn-out everyday ego and can surrender himself to the greater pulsations of the universe.

Laban (1971) refers specifically to dance as:

> a re-establishment of lost and weakened connections with the source of life.

And, more directly relevant to my present point, Shawn (1963) quotes Alger:

> Delsarte translated, in the most compact and precise manner, the metaphysics of the scholastic philosophy into esthetics. And it is something that is as high as the zenith, as deep as the nadir, and as boundless as immensity.

The two great foundation stones upon which Delsarte's cosmic metaphysical system rested, were the Law of Correspondence, and the Law of Trinity. The Law of Correspondence is stated as follows:

> To each spiritual function responds a function of the body; to each grand function of the body corresponds a spiritual act.

Of which Shawn says:

> One must realise that the Law of Correspondence is ever present, simultaneously operating at all times with the Law of Trinity. Each gesture (or tone of voice, inflection and articulation of speech or

song) is expressive of *something*—it is preceded and given birth to by a thought, a feeling, an emotion, a purpose, a design or a motive.

However, such theories involve intractable problems of their own. For, once the issue has been transferred to that sort of metaphysical plane, it is *ipso facto* removed from the plane of intelligible discourse.[1] Yet many writers on expressionism in the arts, and especially on dance, as well as those who write on other aspects of the body-mind problem, appear to be unaware of this consequence of their dependence upon the mystical.

If you tell me that you know that John is in pain because you heard him groaning, that is an understandable reason. It is possible to show that you are wrong, of course, by adducing other reasons which count against your statement, but it can be understood and intelligibly discussed. However, if your claim to know about John's pain depends solely upon a mystical feeling you had about him, then it cannot be understood or intelligibly discussed, and most of us would not be satisifed, even in everyday matters, with claims which could not be backed by cogent reasons. It does seem odd, on the face of it, that when the issues are of greater moment, people are more prepared to indulge in, and accept, metaphysical discourse of this kind. To take a banal example, imagine that you decide to buy a bicycle and go one day to look at what they have in a nearby shop. The salesman approaches and, ignoring the modern machines ranged around, takes you to see an old, rusty one, with spokes missing, a misshapen frame, flat tyres and bent handlebars. "I know it is more expensive than the others," he says, "but it is well worth the extra money. I can assure you that its appearance is deceptive. You can rely upon my mystical feeling that you will find it entirely satisfactory. If you have any trouble with it, that will indicate your own failure to

---

[1] In this respect such theories are in a position similar to those which depend upon intuition, as we shall see in section J (2).

develop the appropriate feeling to appreciate its real quality." This line of sales technique is unlikely to persuade you to buy the bicycle. You would demand some very good reasons in support of the salesman's claims, and your doubts would not be allayed if he waved away your demand, saying that reasons are dull, calculating things, and that we should have more faith in our feelings.

Though this is a mundane and obviously absurd example, a good deal of writing and discussion on more serious issues in fact amounts to no more than this, even if its unintelligibility passes unnoticed. It frequently occurs in relation to the body-mind problem generally, and specifically with respect to expressionism in the arts, especially dance. This is seriously misleading in its implication that involvement with the arts is simply a matter of non-rational emotional reaction. In fact, one needs to develop the capacity to perceive fine distinctions in order to appreciate and respond appropriately to the arts. Correspondingly, to justify a particular interpretation requires thoughtful discrimination. To leave it all to mystical feelings is, in effect, to abandon this demanding, though rewarding task. That is as slipshod in discussion of the arts as it would be in science or mathematics. To give reasons in support of an aesthetic judgment may be different in some respects from giving reasons in other areas of discourse, but we should be clear that to give reasons which ultimately depend upon mysticism is effectively to give no genuine reasons at all, and is therefore no improvement on the traditional theory.

It has been objected against this line of argument that the historical facts are against it, since dance has been related to the mystical throughout the ages. This may well be true, but an appeal to history will not provide the support required to save the credibility of such theories. Mountains, volcanoes, animals, the sun and moon have, in the past, been the objects of religious veneration, and the sources of beliefs about mysterious powers. Similarly, it was believed for centuries that the earth was flat. Yet we do not regard the fact that such beliefs have been firmly held by many generations of people in the past as a valid reason for continuing to hold those beliefs now, in the face of scientific evidence to the contrary. So the historical fact that people have, over a long period, associated dance with the mysterious and occult is no reason for regarding dance as mysterious and occult. If someone proposes an unusual and challenging interpretation of a work of art or artistic performance, he puts himself under an obligation to justify it. It will be no help to be told, for example, "It cannot be discussed. It's all a matter of the inner spirit, a mystical communication between the dancer and me." He can explain his interpretation only by drawing our attention to certain observable features of the dance whose significance we had previously misconstrued, or failed to notice.

However, we should be careful not to assume that it is necessarily, even if it is often, incoherent to interpret a dance or other work of art in terms of inner feelings or mysticism. Such an interpretation may be explicable by reference to what can be seen in the dance itself. As long as it is ultimately answerable to observable features, transcendental or mystical discourse can be unexceptionable. One can explain what is meant by fairy footsteps without relying on a belief in fairies, in terms of lightness and deftness of movement. Drawing attention to such observable phenomena can be understood. What is not intelligible is to leave the explanation in fairyland. It is equally incoherent to leave the justification of an aesthetic judgment in the realm of the transcendental, or mystical feelings. To do so is only less *obviously* absurd than adducing such feelings as standards for judging the relative merits of bicycles. It makes sense to speak of the magic quality of a dance as long as one does not have to be a magician to understand it.

Moreover, though one suspects that some people who adopt obscure terminology do so because they are unable or unwilling to impose upon themselves the self-discipline required for the intricate task of justifying aesthetic judgments, and some appear simply to revel in mysterious word-spinning, it would be wrong to assume that mystical theories should be dismissed as valueless. A point of substance underlies such theories, in the recognition that the connection between body and mind cannot be merely contingent. Faced with the problem of getting at the inner feelings of other people, and realising that we do in fact know about such feelings, the mystic concludes that there must be some sort of transcendentally guaranteed connection. As with the other theories we have examined, his mistake is not a stupid one, and he is not as far from them as might be supposed. Though the behaviourist and the mystic tend to be contemptuous of each other from opposed and apparently irreconcilable positions, they in fact can be seen to share a fallacious presupposition. The behaviourist tends to dismiss aesthetic judgments as irrational because they are not susceptible to his demand for scientific verification—they cannot be substantiated by evidence. The mystic scorns the narrow rigidity of the behaviourist who denies the validity of any claim which cannot be rationally supported. We certainly do have aesthetic and other non-measurable experiences, says the mystic, which are just as valid as scientifically verifiable phenomena.

Notice the shared premiss.

Behaviourist: There is no sound scientific evidence, so it is not rational. Therefore it is nonsense.

Mystic: There is no sound scientific evidence, so it does not come in the sphere of the rational. It is mystical.

The shared premiss is the assumption that if a statement cannot be supported by scientific evidence of some sort, it cannot be rational. But producing such evidence is not the only way of providing rational justification. As we have seen, explanations can be given in terms of reasons as well as of causes. It is characteristic of those who take a serious, informed interest in the arts that their aesthetic judgments *are* supportable by reasons, but that is certainly not to say that such support is given by scientific tests and measurement. The mystic recognises the fallacy of taking behavioural evidence as equivalent to a mind. He also recognises the impossibility of taking such evidence as contingently related to a mind. He correctly insists that nothing short of a guaranteed connection between body and mind will do, but a mystical guarantee, by its very nature, transcends intelligible discourse, and is therefore no guarantee at all.

E:

CRITERIA

(1) In general

What will guarantee the connection between physical behaviour and mental experience? The only possibility is some sort of logical connection. It has to be shown that the relationship is neither contingent nor mystical, but rather a matter of the logic of the concepts concerned. Pain behaviour, for example, must be more than a sign of pain—the connection must be such that the very concept of pain would be unintelligible apart from this sort of behaviour. Yet at first sight, as we have seen, it does not seem possible that there can be a logical relationship, for, despite his pain behaviour, it is always possible that John is not in pain—he may be pretending. Therefore pain behaviour is not logically sufficient to guarantee pain. This point is well understood by both the traditionalist and the mystic. Each recognises that writhing and groaning do not logically imply that there is an experience of pain, hence each tries to suggest other types of relationship. The mistake in this way of looking at the matter is to take too limited a view of what it is to be a logical relationship. There is a common and oversimple assumption that there is only one sort of logical connection, which is concerned with inexorable deductive steps towards inescapable conclusions. For example:

All men are mortal.
Socrates is a man.
Therefore Socrates is mortal.

The conclusion is inescapable, given the premisses. No wedge can be driven between them and the conclusion, so there is no possibility of error. But, though we certainly do not have a logical connection of this sort between physical behaviour and mental experience, we do not need to accept that this is the only type of logical relationship there can be. Another type of logical connection is that of a criterion. I shall use the term "criterion" in the way in which, if I understand him correctly, Wittgenstein intended it in his later work. This is a somewhat contentious issue, but the details of it need not concern us, especially since, at a later stage, the term will be used in a wider sense than that which I take to be Wittgenstein's.

To say that X is a criterion of Y means that the presence of X is necessarily a reason for the presence of Y. So that if someone observes X, has no other reason which counts against it, yet denies Y, then he simply does not understand the concept of Y. Thus, for example, if you see John writhing and groaning in the circumstances of a road accident, and you have no reason to suspect, say, that he is pretending, then such behaviour is sufficient to justify your saying that John is in pain. That is, such behaviour is a criterion of pain.

This notion of a criterion is best understood, perhaps, by contrasting it with evidence. Consider this example.

I look out of the window at the front of the house and see that the pavements are glistening. The tennis players, who have been playing on the courts opposite, are covering their rackets and leaving the courts. People walking along the road are putting up umbrellas, donning raincoats, turning up collars. Through the window at the back of the house I notice widening circles in the garden pond. All this is good evidence that it is raining. I have good reason to believe, from my experience and that of others, that people put up umbrellas and so forth when it is raining. Nevertheless such evidence is indirect. It depends upon an observed and well-attested correlation. Moreover, as in the case where the evidence of the turning windmill sails justifies my assumption that the wind is blowing, it is open to me to check the correlation directly. And we have seen the importance of recognising that indirect ways of finding out depend ultimately upon direct methods. If I put my hand out of the window and feel sensations as of cold, wet drops, I discover directly that it is raining. So I know indirectly from the *evidence* of raincoats and umbrellas, and directly from the sensations of wet, cold drops, which are the *criteria* of rain.

It would be quite possible to understand what rain is without knowing that people put up umbrellas when rain is falling. Umbrellas have nothing directly to do with the meaning of "It is raining." Someone, for example, from a country in which umbrellas are not used might know very well what rain is, yet when he looks out of the window he might be puzzled to notice that the people walking past are hiding under strange mushroom-shaped objects. But if someone walks outside and feels the sensations of cold, wet drops, and does not know that it is raining, he simply does not understand what it means to say it is raining.

The various pieces of evidence which I saw through the window are not directly connected with the meaning of the term. In order to teach someone who had never encountered it what "rain" means, we should not refer to umbrellas, raincoats and scurrying tennis players. We should take him to feel the cold, wet drops, which are the criteria. To put the same point another way, "It is raining," if true, does not imply that there are umbrellas etc. whereas it does imply that there are cold, wet drops.

It should be noticed that even in the case of illusion, the same criteria are involved. That is, an illusion of rain depends ultimately upon illusory criteria. Understanding a concept and knowing how to employ it are independent of illusion and reality.

The distinction between criteria and evidence may be understood as a distinction between the most direct, and various indirect ways of knowing that something is present or true. Thus, though unexceptionable in some respects, Shoemaker's explanation (1963) may be misleading. He says that X is a criterion of Y if X is "direct, non-inductive evidence in favour of the truth of Y." Though it is true that a criterial connection is direct and non-inductive, to use the term "evidence" may be confusing, since it is normally used of a quite different, contingent, sort of relationship. And many of the errors of the theories we have discussed stem from a failure to appreciate precisely this distinction.

Yet, to repeat the point, though a criterion is necessarily a reason for, it does not have to be logically sufficient for. I lean out of the window, and on the basis of the criteria—the cold, wet drop-sensations—I am justified in assuming that it is raining, but I could still be wrong. It might be that Jenny, the naughty little girl from next door, is sitting on the roof with a watering can, playing her latest little mischievous trick on me. Nevertheless, it is still true that there is no other ultimate, direct way of finding out whether it is raining than by reference to the criteria. And, as we have seen, indirect methods are always answerable to direct methods. There were various indirect ways of discovering the score at Wimbledon—for example by telephoning or turning on the radio, but these depend ultimately upon the direct method available to the spectators on Centre Court. Similarly, the writhing and groaning of the road accident victim are criteria of his being in pain. Such behaviour is necessarily a reason for our judgment that he is in pain, even though it is possible that he is pretending. Given the relevant circumstances it is possible that some people, sometimes, can pretend to be in pain, but not that all or most people all or most of the time should pretend to be in pain.

Criteria, then, are reasons which provide a logical connection, in this case between behaviour statements and mental-experience statements. Furthermore, it should be noticed that criteria are publicly observable.

However, there are many who would deny that a criterion, in this sense, can be regarded as a logical guarantee. Such people tend to insist that a logical relationship must attain the irrefutable standard of certainty of a deductive conclusion. But this distortingly restricts the varied character of logical implications. For example, contrast

"All men are mortal"
with
"The average British family has 2.4 children."

The former is incompatible with any particular man being immortal, whereas the latter is not incompatible with any particular family having a different number of children—indeed, no family could have exactly 2.4 children. So the logical character of the latter statement is different from that of the former. Nevertheless, though the logical limits set by the former are more rigid, it is still true that there *are* logical limits set by the latter. If the average family has 2.4 children there are limits, for instance, to the number of families which have no children or twenty children.

Similarly, it is a logical point that there could be no language if most people most of the time told lies. But that is not to say that it is logically impossible to tell lies. Logical relationships are not all of the same type.

Now we are in a position to understand more clearly certain aspects of the arguments which were discussed above. It was said that there is a sense in which the behaviourist is right to say that mental statements can be understood only by reference to physical behaviour. He would be right if he meant by this that the actions of other people are *criteria* of their mental experiences. Instead, he mistakenly construes behaviour as *evidence*. Understood as evidence, physical behaviour cannot lead to conclusions about minds, and since there is no other evidence of their existence, this quite naturally leads the behaviourist to deny that there are mental experiences.

The traditionalist makes the mistake of regarding behaviour as evidence, but he also insists that there are mental experiences, and this is what makes his theory untenable. For there is no coherent way of reaching conclusions about mental experiences from behaviour, if the behaviour is taken to be evidence.

To say that there is no evidence of mental experiences is not to say that people do not have them, for that would be to deny that people are ever sad, happy, in pain. Wittgenstein (1953 § 304) imagines a questioner who has not grasped this point, asking:

"But you will surely admit that there is a difference between pain-behaviour accompanied by pain and pain-behaviour without any pain?"

Wittgenstein replies:

"Admit it? What greater difference could there be?"

Questioner:

"And yet you again and again reach the conclusion that the sensation is a nothing."

Wittgenstein:

"Not at all. It is not a *something,* but not a *nothing* either! The conclusion was only that a nothing would serve just as well as a something about which nothing could be said. We have only rejected the grammar which tries to force itself on us here."

The mistaken "grammar" is that of taking the behaviour as a sign or evidence of pain. But the sensation cannot be identified apart from the behavioural criteria. That is, apart from the criteria there is no way even of referring to the sensation. If we try to separate the experience of pain from the pain behaviour by regarding the behaviour as *evidence*, then the mental experience becomes a something about which nothing can be said.

We can now more clearly understand the error of the scientist who thought that low blood pressure could be identified with sadness. He made the mistake of assuming that behaviour is evidence, just like low blood pressure. But to obtain his correlation he has to discover that his subject is sad on the basis not of evidence but of criteria. Sobbing, frowning, hanging one's head, sighing etc. are not evidence of sadness, they are criteria, and another criterion is what the person himself says. This, as we have seen, is by no means decisive, or logically sufficient. We may know from other criteria that what the person says about his own feelings is deliberately misleading or mistaken. Nevertheless, his statement about his own feelings is a criterion. We should beware of the tendency to draw a sharp boundary between verbal and non-verbal behaviour. The scientist could not begin to obtain evidence unless he understood the criteria for sadness, and the subject's report is one of these.

Similarly, expressive movements in dance are criteria of the emotions which are being expressed. There is no other way of referring to these particular emotions. This is what was meant by saying that the emotion is in the movement itself. If we take the movement to be evidence of, or to be standing for, the emotion which is being expressed, we thereby create a gap between the movement and the emotion—a gap which either runs us into the problems of the traditional view, or inclines us to the behaviourist view that to overcome those problems we have to deny the experience of emotion.

It now becomes clear why we had to achieve a satisfactory theory of meaning before we could begin to appreciate how a movement can be expressive. To be in the grip of the naming theory of meaning inhibits the possibility of understanding expression in any form. If we take the meaning of the word "sad", or the meaning of a sad movement, to be the emotion which it stands for, then the word or movement expresses a something about which nothing can be said. The confusion is brought about by the assumption that meaning is naming, that expressive movement has meaning only if it stands for the relevant emotion. To construe the grammar in this way is to create an impassable gulf between name and object, between evidence and that for which it is evidence.

Expressive movements do not stand for anything, they are not evidence for anything. They are *criteria* of the emotions which they express. And this is true not only of expression in the art of movement, but also of expression in the arts generally.

The position can be summarised in this way:

Pain statements cannot be reduced to behaviour statements.

Pain statements cannot be reached by means of statements about behavioural evidence.

Pain statements are given their meaning by behavioural criteria.

> You learned the *concept* pain when you learned the language. (Wittgenstein 1953 § 384).

And what is true of the concept of pain is equally true of emotion concepts. The relation between behaviour and mental experience, between physical movement and what it expresses, is a conceptual, a logical relation, it is a matter of the logic of the concepts concerned.

> For the characteristic mark of all 'feelings' is that there is expression of them, i.e. facial expression, gestures, of feeling.

> And just try to think over something very sad with an expression of radiant joy. (Wittgenstein 1967 § § 513 and 508).

The impossibility of thinking over something very sad while expressing radiant joy is not a contingent but a logical impossibility, in a suitably broad sense of that term.

E:

CRITERIA

(2) Of emotions

The discussion so far has been primarily in terms of sensations, for expository purposes, but we need now to examine the notion of criteria specifically in relation to the emotions, for to be clear about this is of the first importance to an understanding of expression in movement. It is illuminating to compare sensations and emotions by drawing attention to two opposite, plausible, but equally misleading tendencies:

(a) to identify emotions with certain sensations.
(b) to create too wide a division between them.

Of these the former appears to be the more common. Certain sensations undoubtedly are important features of some emotions. When someone becomes very angry or terrified, for example, there are physical changes in his face, his pulse-rate increases, he may perspire and have sensations such as a dry throat. Similarly, acute embarrassment induces blushing and various other uncomfortable sensations. It is natural to assume that such sensations and physical changes actually constitute the emotion concerned. Support for this notion seems to come from the fact that one does indeed experience emotion—one *feels* angry, afraid, embarrassed. This in turn can easily lead to the idea that by measuring bodily changes one can identify and measure the intensity of emotions. We have already considered the case of the scientist who wanted to identify sadness with low blood pressure. We found that though correlations may be discovered between degree of bodily changes and intensity of emotion, that is certainly not to say that in measuring the former we are measuring the latter. For we have to know in some way other than by scientific tests that a person is in a certain emotional state before we can even begin to try to establish the correlation.

There is the further consideration that in fact the extreme cases cited above are by no means typical of the whole range of emotions. It may be plausible to suggest that fear of snakes or spiders can be measured by psychogalvanic reflex. The subject of the experiment is suitably wired and connected to the relevant instruments, a snake is produced before him and the reading on the scale or graph indicates the degree of his reaction. But we need to be aware of the differences in emotional reactions. Tests of this sort are inapplicable even to a wide variety of other cases of fear, let alone other emotions. How, for example, could one measure in the same way the fear that the increasing influx of commuting or retired Londoners will hasten the extinction of many interesting Sussex traditions?

This tendency to believe that it is necessary to examine characteristic sensations in order accurately to locate what is essential to an emotion, may be seen as another variant of the definitional view of meaning. There is an inclination to ask "What is emotion?" and, as in other cases we considered, the form of the question already limits the sort of answer which can be given. We seem impelled to try to find the essential core of the concept concerned, so, just as there was a tendency to concentrate on extreme cases of expecting, in our earlier example, so, in the present case, we are inclined to concentrate our attention on examples of intense emotional reactions in order to discover what is essential to emotions. We ask "What is fear?" or "What is the essence of fear?" and it is evident that certain sensations and bodily changes always seem to occur in, and to be importantly bound up with, occasions of extreme fear. It is understandably easy to assume from this that such sensations and bodily changes just *are* the emotions, or at least that they are essential features of emotions generally.

A contributory factor is the temptation to assume that to discover the true nature of anything we need to examine it closely, but this is not always true. To discover the shape of a mountain range we have to move away from it. And we shall fail to appreciate the meaning of a painting if we walk up very close to it and concentrate exclusively upon the minute details of what are supposed to be the most important features of it. Similarly, to concentrate more and more closely upon the feelings of people who are experiencing, or who have recently experienced fear, in order to come to an understanding of the concept of fear, is to be looking in the wrong direction. Indeed there is a good sense in which it is precisely the opposite direction to that in which we should be looking. Elizabeth Anscombe (1958) makes the point in this way:

> That is why looking for the meaning of 'anger' in what a man feels who feels angry yields such dissatisfying results, as if the anger itself had slipped between our fingers and we are left with details which, while relevant, do not add up to anger.

Yet we should beware of making the opposite mistake, mentioned above, of making too wide a separation of sensations from emotions, since in some cases sensations and bodily changes are important characteristics of emotions, especially of intense emotions. We cannot imagine violent rage or extreme anxiety unaccompanied by certain sensations and physical changes. The behaviour of the angry man, and the sensations he experiences—eyes blazing, lips trembling, heart pounding, etc.—cannot be merely contingently related to his anger, for that would involve the insuperable difficulties of the traditional view, by separating behaviour and sensations from the emotion of anger.

It is tempting to conclude from these considerations that just as groaning and writhing are criteria of pain, so shaking fists and experiencing certain sensations are criteria of anger. But the case of emotions is more complex, and this, it will appear, has a significant bearing upon an understanding of how it is that emotions can be expressed in the arts. First, in order to make plain what is involved in the notion of criteria as applied to the emotions, we need to examine in more detail the relation between them and sensations.

Though importantly related to some emotions, sensations cannot be identified with those emotions for at least two reasons:

(a) It is in principle possible to produce the sensations characteristic, for example, of extreme fear in some way other than by creating frightening circumstances. It would be possible to achieve this by drugs or means of electrical apparatus, but it is obviously not true that simply as a consequence of experiencing these sensations the subject is afraid.

(b) It might be that someone happens to have a particular sensation, say an itch, whenever he is in extreme danger—indeed this might be found to be true of most people, but this is a contingent matter, it is not part of the concept of fear.

Frequently people say that when they are extremely frightened they feel as if they have lumps in the throat, yet this sensation also commonly occurs when people are sad. Indeed it is not necessarily indicative of any emotion at all, since it could be a symptom of tonsillitis or some other ailment. So the problem is to explain how it is that a sensation can be characteristic specifically of extreme fear when it is not limited to that or even to any emotion. It will help us to solve this problem if we consider an actual case. A man who has recently been in great danger tells us that, as usual in such circumstances, he had the sensation of lumps in his throat. We want to discover how this sensation can be conceptually related to his fear, and not just a matter of chance. So we ask him how he knows it is a fear sensation. To answer the question he would tend naturally to give us an account of the *whole context.* "My toe holds suddenly broke away, and I was left clinging to the overhanging rock face by my finger tips, dangling over a sheer drop of two thousand feet, my heart thumping wildly, lumps in my throat . . ."

To take into account the whole circumstance of his experiencing the sensation in this way is not incidental. On the contrary, if we concentrate solely upon what the man was feeling we shall be unable to understand his sensations as, precisely, those of fear. For sensations and patterns of behaviour are recognisable as emotional only if they normally occur in appropriate circumstances. So we have to take a wider view and include the situation in which they occurred. And a criterial element in this wider context is the object of the emotion. That is, we recognise behaviour as emotion-behaviour, and sensations as emotion-sensations, only because in normal circumstances they are directed in certain ways at an object. (This point was made rather effectively in a comedy film I saw recently, in which one of the characters said, "I had this strange sensation in my throat and stomach, and I knew I was either in love or had chicken pox.")

The need to take account of context is not enough by itself to differentiate emotions, for this may be necessary even in the case of sensations. A man's writhing and groaning are criteria which allow us to say that we know he is in pain, but it is by no means irrelevant to our judgment that he is lying in the road, near a car which has just skidded violently etc. On the other hand an actor playing Gloster in *King Lear,* in the scene where his eyes are plucked out, may also writhe and groan, but we know that he is not in pain since his behaviour occurs on a stage as part of a play. Thus, though context may be more important in the case of emotions, it is certainly relevant to sensations. However, an emotion, unlike a sensation, normally requires an object. Contrast:

(a) As John walked along he felt a sudden stab of pain.
with
(b) As John walked along he felt a sudden stab of anger.

There is a sense in which the former statement is complete as it stands, whereas one feels one needs to know at what John felt angry One needs to be given a context which includes an object at which the anger is directed. Similarly, one is afraid of snakes, angered by impertinence, bored with trivial conversation, saddened at the loss of a friend, amused by repartee.

A misunderstanding of this characteristic of emotion-concepts might arise here. Some philosophers in the past have recognised that emotions are more than just sensations or behaviour. They appreciated that sensations, for example, have to be directed on to an object in order to be emotional. This led them to postulate a cognitive element, which was thought to be an image in the mind of the person experiencing the emotion, which directed the sensations towards the object. It was believed, for example, that John has anger-sensations and concurrently has a mental image of the object of his anger. But this view is open to objections similar to those we brought against the traditional view. It would be possible, on this account, to have the wrong image and hence direct one's emotion at the wrong object. For example, John might be angry because a thief has just stolen his recently acquired gold watch, but perhaps the first image which comes to his mind on discovering the theft is that of his wife's distress, since she gave him the watch. In that case on this hypothesis he would be angry not with the thief but with his wife.

So a contingent association, one which just happens to obtain, between emotion and object, is not enough. The relation has to be a matter of logic. Wittgenstein says (1967 § 489).

The language game "I am afraid" already contains the object.

Wittgenstein is pointing out that to understand the sentence "I am afraid" one needs to appreciate that it normally has an object even if on particular occasions it lacks one. That is, it is part of the *concept* of fear that it normally has an object. This allows for secondary or derivative cases such as a feeling of nameless dread. One may wake up with such a feeling yet be unable to say, at least for a time, of what one feels afraid. Such feelings are recognisable as feelings of fear only because they normally occur in a situation where they are directed on to an object.

In the case of behaviour, too, there must normally be something in the environment which is a target for the emotion in order for it to be recognisable as emotion behaviour. For example, we might notice a group of horses running wildly round a field, rearing up on their hind legs and neighing. If we did not know them, and with no further information than this, we should be at a loss to understand their behaviour. It might be that about this time every day their owner comes to feed them some sugar lumps, and they become excited at the prospect. They may simply be young and frisky in a blustery wind, or have caught the scent of mares in the next field. Or their behaviour could even be the result of a drug. But if we notice a rather savage-looking dog, barking and running after them, snapping at their legs, we should probably conclude that the horses are afraid. Their behaviour is now recognisable as fear-behaviour because it can be seen that it is directed on to the dog. One could not understand the actions of the horses as criteria of fear without identifying the object.

Of course it is possible to know that an animal is afraid without knowing of what it is afraid. This is a derivative case, like that of waking up with a feeling of unidentifiable dread—it depends upon our having observed the animal, or other animals, in situations where an object of the emotional reaction is identifiable. When we have learned that an animal reacts in a certain way whenever it is confronted with a frightening object, we can then recognise similar behaviour patterns as characteristic of fear even where there is no obvious candidate for the object of the emotion. Similarly a very young child may behave in a way which shows that he is very distressed—screaming, sobbing, writhing about vigorously. In isolation such behaviour is insufficient to allow us to understand it. He may be in pain, but equally he may be terrified or in a temper. For his actions to be recognisable as emotional we need to know the context, and especially at which particular object the behaviour is directed.

We saw earlier that in general there is a conceptual relation between physical behaviour and mental experience, that we get to mental experience by means of behavioural criteria. It now emerges that in the specific case of emotions we get to the mental experience by means of behavioural criteria in a context which includes the object of behaviour. We know that someone is feeling certain sensations by behavioural criteria. The connection between the sensations characteristic of an emotion, and the object of it, is a matter of the concept of emotion. Thus emotion-sensations are logically related to their objects. The relation between object and emotion is internal to the concept of emotion itself, so that an emotional response could not normally be understood as such in the absence of the object.

Emotions, then, are more complex than sensations. The criteria are not simply patterns of behaviour, but sensations or patterns of behaviour in a context which includes an object to which they are directed.

F:

REASONS

(1) Reason and emotion

We are now in a position to examine a difference between sensations and emotions which is a consequence of the foregoing discussion and which is of considerable significance to an understanding of expression in movement and in the arts generally. This difference concerns seeing and giving reasons for one thing rather than another as the object of an emotion.

There is a tendency to overlook the fact that emotions, unlike sensations, can be justifiable or unjustifiable, reasonable or unreasonable. It would make no sense to tell someone that it is unreasonable of him to be in pain, and we cannot normally affect his sensation by giving him reasons to show that it is inappropriate (though we might, of course, induce him to bear his pain more courageously). But we can point out to someone that he is wrong to become angry, or that his fear is groundless, by giving reasons which may have a substantial effect on his emotional feelings. Yet, despite the fact that such an experience is common enough, there is a widespread misunderstanding about the possibility of giving reasons for emotions, which is revealed in the mistaken belief that there is a great gulf fixed between reason and emotion, in that if something is a matter of emotional feelings it is often held to have nothing to do with reason. This misunderstanding is largely a consequence of a prevalent but oversimple view of the character of reasoning, which is implicitly restricted to the sort of procedure which takes place in deductive logic or science. It is true that, where the emotions are concerned, we do not usually have a procedure which involves a series of steps of argument, each following logically from the previous one, nor do we always achieve decisive conclusions, but, contrary to popular belief, not all reasoning has to incorporate these features. It may be less misleading, at least in most cases, to regard emotional feelings as answerable to reasoned argument, in a sense to be explained.

There are at least two types of reasons which are characteristically given for emotions which, though they are not always sharply distinguishable, may be broadly classified as:

(a) moral
(b) interpretative

In clear-cut cases of the former it is not the character of the emotion concerned which is primarily in question, but rather the moral justification of it. Thus, for example, a teacher may feel annoyed with a pupil who is persistently late for school, and if he were asked why he felt like that he would be able to point out the general desirability of punctuality, and in particular the disruption caused to himself and to the other pupils in a class when someone comes in after a lesson has begun. Justifying, commending, explaining emotional feelings by reference to moral attitudes in this way is by no means unusual, but the full implications of giving reasons of this sort are not sufficiently appreciated. It is frequently not recognised, for example, that the terms "reasonable" and "unreasonable," and their cognates, are themselves commonly used in a morally evaluative sense.

Where moral reasons are given with respect to emotional reactions, their strength is derived from the fundamental attitudes of the person who gives them, and when two people have very different moral attitudes, each may give a conflicting but equally sound set of reasons for and against, respectively, the feeling at issue.

Consider a hypothetical dispute between Martin and Mary. Martin advocates a much more liberal and progressive attitude towards sexual freedom, which would not discourage relationships with a variety of partners, and would include incestuous and homosexual relationships where desired. The only thing which prevents a natural enjoyment of such relationships, he argues, is the anachronistic prejudice of the many people who refuse to think about the issue with an open mind, and who perpetuate the unnecessary and often harmful repression of sexual desires from the age of puberty which has bedevilled society for so long. Mary is disgusted to hear such views expressed and justifies her feelings by giving reasons which refer to what she regards as the degenerate sort of society which would be the result of a general acceptance of Martin's views. She believes his attitude to be not liberal and progressive, but permissive, retrogressive and thoroughly unreasonable. Yet to Martin, it is Mary's reaction which is unreasonable, a narrow-minded determination to cling unthinkingly to outmoded conventions, even though reliable contraception, for example, has removed the need for the sexual restrictions incorporated into earlier moral codes.

The issue between them is unlikely to be settled by further discussion, for in a moral dispute, though each party may be able to adduce good reasons, that does not mean that there is necessarily a decisive solution to be found if only they are sufficiently open-minded and go on searching for it long enough. Two sets of opposing reasons may be equally sound and internally consistent but the soundness of each is drawn solely from the underlying moral attitude which it encapsulates. Thus where the fundamental moral attitudes are quite different, the reasons given for opposing views carry no weight, and no solution will be possible. But there is no need to go to the other extreme and assume that moral disagreements can never be resolved. One may be able to point out that someone's moral argument is self-contradictory, or that the implications of it would lead to a position which its proponent would not wish to uphold, or which he would find embarrassing, because of its conflict with one or more of his principles. Moreover, one is sometimes convinced by the strength of the reasons given for an opposing point of view, in which case, if one is honest, one has to concede that one was wrong. Perhaps one reacted angrily, and felt entirely justified in doing so, but later one comes to appreciate that not all the circumstances had been taken into consideration, so one had been unfair. The possibility of reaching agreement in this way depends upon certain common assumptions or some measure of shared fundamental moral attitudes to which implicit or explicit appeal can be made. Where there is very little underlying agreement there may be no way of resolving the issue. It is a matter of degree, the less the overlap of fundamental belief, the less the possibility of reaching agreement. Indeed, without some overlap of moral content one cannot even understand another's argument as a moral argument. So that, at a deeper level, paradoxical as it may sound, without some measure of agreement there cannot even be genuine disagreement, for where there is no common underlying belief one will simply fail to see that the other is giving reasons.

There is much more than this to be said about moral reasoning, but it is sufficient for our present purposes to appreciate something of its character and to recognise that emotional feelings are very often importantly answerable to and affected by such reasons.

However, it is the latter type of reason-giving, which I have called interpretative, which is of greater significance for understanding expression in movement. It includes attempting to discern or convey the salient features of certain patterns of behaviour in its relation to an object in order to appreciate the emotional character of it. This is how we are able to become aware of mistakes in identifying our own emotional states as it dawns on us that our feelings and behavioural tendencies are not what we had assumed them to be. I might have misconstrued my own feelings until I notice, or someone points out, the significance of some aspect of my behaviour which I had previously overlooked and which now sheds a new light on my emotion. Where these two types of reasoning are clearly separable, this type is different from the former in that it is not a matter of the moral justification of feelings but of what feelings they are. For example, consider once again a situation where we are watching a group of horses in a field who are behaving in a very disturbed fashion. This time, though there is a dog in the vicinity he seems amiable enough, and is sniffing in the hedgerow, apparently oblivious of the horses. There is no immediately obvious way of describing their behaviour so we may come to different conclusions. It may still be fear of the dog, but it may be fear of something else, or eager anticipation of being fed with sugar lumps, or simply excitement induced by a high wind. Each of these interpretations may be supportable by reasons which cite certain aspects of their behaviour as significantly related to one object rather than another. Such reasons may show that one description is more convincing than the others, but on the other hand there may be nothing to choose between two possible interpretations, no aspect of the situation which can be pointed out as decisively tipping the scales in favour of one. So that, in this type of case too, the fact that good reasons can be given does not imply that there is only one correct answer, for an opposing view may be supported by equally good reasons.

It must be stressed again that in many cases these two types of reasoning are inextricably linked, for very often it is how one sees the object which determines one's feelings and one's moral attitude. For example, the teacher who felt annoyed by his pupil's unpunctuality may be given reasons which show that the lateness was unavoidable—perhaps because the boy had to help his crippled father to work every day before coming to school. If the teacher now sees the object not as irresponsible behaviour but as commendably considerate behaviour, his feelings will change accordingly. Similarly, Othello was given reasons by Iago for seeing Desdemona's behaviour as evidence of infidelity, and this, he believed, justified his intense jealousy. But, too late, he is given further reasons which make him realise that Iago had deliberately misled him, and that Desdemona's actions were innocent. The change of object from unfaithful behaviour to blameless behaviour corresponds to a change in Othello's feelings from jealousy to remorse, and this is brought about by appreciating the significance of reasons which throw a new light on the actions of Desdemona and Iago. One could easily think of many other instances in which appreciating the reasons given for a different way of seeing a situation can have a considerable effect on the way we feel about it.

What makes many people feel that they have to deny that reasons can be in any way relevant to emotions is the common belief that in any controversy where genuine reasoning is employed it is possible, at least in principle, to reach a correct, universally decisive conclusion, and, as we have seen, this is not always possible where there is a disagreement about the character or justification of emotions. We considered in section E (1) the tendency to restrict what can be counted as a truly logical relationship, and this limited notion of reasoning, is similar to and usually connected with it. Deductive and to a lesser extent inductive reasoning, as used in mathematics and science, are regarded as the only kinds worthy of the name, and any other pretender is held to be at best peripheral, and at worst merely subjective, since it cannot produce the concrete, definitive conclusions of these paradigms.

One certainly would not wish to deny that deductive and inductive procedures are central examples of reasoning, but it is a mistake to take them as the norms to which other kinds must closely approximate if they are to be regarded as legitimate. In fact both moral and interpretative reasoning are also central examples, rather than peripheral ones. We should resist the common tendency to take too narrow a range of paradigms as the norm, examples of which we saw when extreme cases of fear and expecting were considered in order to find the essential qualities of the concepts concerned. Those who argue in this way appear to be unaware that there are different sorts of reasoning. Furthermore they overlook the fact that even their paradigm disciplines depend upon reasoning very similar to that of seeing and describing certain patterns of behaviour as emotional.

Not all mathematics, by any means, consists of following deductive steps to inevitable conclusions. Often the problems in higher mathematics are of a very different character. Given a certain set of agreed facts the mathematician has to try to find a theory which will bring them together under an interpretation, and sometimes there is a disagreement about the theoretical basis of facts which are not themselves the subject of dispute. Similarly, not all science consists of conducting experiments and observations, for very often the scientist is faced with the problem of how to interpret the results of his research, which may be rather different from what he had anticipated. In such cases as these the reasons which contribute to the proposal of a particular conclusion are often disparate, and would more readily suggest the metaphor of the net than the chain of reasoning which is associated with the deductive method. A physicist, for example, may propose a higher-level theory which subsumes several lower-level ones under a single, comprehensive explanatory system. And we should notice that here too disagreements as to the respective merits of rival hypotheses may be impossible to resolve in the absence of further information. So that deductive and inductive procedures which lead to decisive conclusions are not the only types of reasoning employed even in mathematics and science.

Indeed, one can go further than this, for there is a sense in which the possibility of classification according to a theory is a necessary precondition of discovering any fact. Sir Karl Popper, the eminent philosopher of science, insists that the scientist inevitably sets out on each of his enquiries with a general hypothesis which he then subjects to searching empirical tests. He sets out to find *something,* which is not, of course, to say that he doesn't have an open mind about the results of his research. But it is to say that the notion of the "ideally" open mind, of the scientist who simply conducts random experiments with no thought as to their possible outcome, until certain conclusions reveal themselves, is radically mistaken. Any fact is a fact only in relation to some theoretical background which, being itself logically prior to deductive and inductive reasoning, cannot be arrived at by those methods of reasoning. So far from the scientific method providing a touchstone of concrete, irrefutable reasoning, which produces facts which are true for all time, Popper shows that it is a mark of a genuine scientific theory that it is *falsifiable*.

Hermann Bondi, Professor of Applied Mathematics, and distinguished theoretical astronomer, comments (1972):

> I regard the very use of the word 'fact' as misleading, because 'fact' is an emotive word which suggests something hard and firm. What we have in science is always a jumble of observation, understanding of the equipment with which the observation was carried out, interpretation and analysis. We can never clear one from another. Certain experiments that were interpreted in a particular way in their day we now interpret quite differently—but they might well have been claimed as 'facts' in those days . . . It's important to realise that in science it isn't a question of who is right and who is wrong: it is much more a question of who is useful, who is stimulating, who has helped things forward. Even after very many tests a theory remains provisional. For example, Newton's theory of gravitation was not only regarded as right: it was considered unthinkable that it could be otherwise. It was only at the very end of the 19th century, with yet more refined observation and analysis, that people began to suspect the theory ever so slightly. Now we know that it is no longer a tenable theory.

So the kind of reasoning which involves grasping or trying to point out the significance of certain interpretations or explanatory conjectures is by no means a degenerate, subjective and unreliable form of reasoning. On the contrary, the paradigms with which it is unflatteringly compared, indeed any academic discipline, may be said ultimately to depend on it too.

But this brings to light a confusion, for to call it subjective and unreliable is implicitly to measure it against a standard of what it is believed reasoning ought to be. And that involves the commonly encountered mistake of inadvertently crossing the wires, of trying to apply the standards of one form of reasoning to another. To say that interpretative reasoning is vague and unreliable because it cannot attain the certainty of deductive conclusions is a confusion of this sort. For interpretative reasoning is not deductive reasoning, hence the standards of the latter cannot coherently be applied to it. To fail to appreciate this point would be like denying that roses can be of much value since they don't taste very good. Yet it is this implicit and incoherent measurement against an inappropriate paradigm which is largely responsible for the popular belief that what is a matter of feeling cannot be a matter of reason, and must therefore be justified by resort to the metaphysical. We need to be aware that there are various forms of reasoning, which may be similar in some ways, but are different in others, and it is a confusion to try to assimilate them all to one or two central types.

Interpretative reasoning does not depend upon inner feelings and it is not subjective. It consists of accounting for aspects of the situation under consideration in such a way as to bring them under a certain pattern of comprehension. It is by reference to such reasons, implicitly or explicitly, that we are able to understand emotionally expressive movement or behaviour, by seeing it under a description in the context of its occurrence, and this will include appreciating the significance of the object towards which it is directed.

It might be objected that in many cases behaviour is so obviously recognisable that there can be no scope for interpretation and reasoning. There is a sense in which it does seem odd to talk of interpreting the actions of a man who is running across a field chased by a ferocious-looking bull, or those of a person who is clearly in pain or very depressed. But these are cases of very obvious interpretation rather than none. The reasons for the way we see the situation are simply taken for granted, so that we are not even aware of them. Yet, though *in fact* there may be no doubt, no particular interpretation is *logically* compelling, however overwhelming the tendency to see it in only one way. It is always possible to be mistaken even in such a case as that of the man being chased across a field by a bull. He may be an even more eccentric pet-lover than most Englishmen, who has managed to tame the animal and teach it to run round the field after him. Now of course this would be a quite extraordinary event, but it is not an impossible one.

However, though no interpretation is logically compelling, we should avoid the temptation to think that there can be such a thing as behaviour under *no* interpretation. This is a species of the common belief, often revealed, for example, in discussion of the psychology of perception, that there are bare, neutral facts, as it were, out there in the objective world, and the interpretation of them is a sort of supervenient icing on the cake. But this is incoherent, for what we take to be a fact *is* the way we interpret it, it is a fact only from some point of view. We can change the way we see behaviour and other phenomena, but we cannot project ourselves out of the realm of interpretation altogether and consider them from some ideally objective, unconceptualised position.

Kant (1929) puts the same point in this way:

> Thoughts without contents are empty,
> Intuitions without concepts are blind.

What Kant means is that it is unintelligible to think that there can be interpretation without something to which it applies, or something which is not interpreted in some way or other. There cannot be a concept which is not a concept of something, and there cannot be a thing which is not classified somehow. It is difficult even to put this point since to talk about something which is not classified at all is to talk about a something about which nothing can be said. So the obviousness of the correct description of certain sorts of behaviour lends no support to the argument that no reasons could be adduced for seeing them in this way rather than another. And anyway some conclusions in mathematics and science are equally obvious, yet no one, presumably, would want to deny that reasons could be given to justify them.

In short, to give reasons for seeing behaviour as emotional consists of drawing attention to those aspects of it which bring it under a particular description, of which the most significant factor is the object which one takes to be criterially related to it. For to argue that the behaviour is directed onto a different object is to argue for a different criterion, and therefore, in an important sense, for a different emotion.

F:

REASONS

(2) Reasoning and expressive movement in dance

It is a central theme of this book that popular talk, and indeed many theories of expression and meaning in the arts, especially dance, are vitiated by an underlying confusion about the emotions, which I have called the traditional theory.[1] We have already exposed its internal incoherence and we can now go on to see how it creates difficulties for understanding the arts. It can be shown that, though it is commonly accepted without question, it implies a position which few would want to accept, for it would follow that the arts, like the emotions in general, could not be intelligibly discussed. And even those who hold the traditional dualist view usually contradict that view pragmatically, in that they exchange opinion about the arts as freely as anyone else. As an example, consider the dilemma in which a teacher of dance, imbued with the traditional theory, would find herself if she were to trace out the consequences of it, though we should remember that the same issue of principle would apply in the other art forms.

[1] Casey (1966) has applied some similar philosophical points to criticism of English literature.

113

One horn of the dilemma is a very natural conviction of the importance of individual emotional response, which might be expressed as follows:

> It is the spontaneous feeling for dance which is of paramount importance. Aesthetic meaning, and the aesthetic quality of movement, are what each performer or spectator experiences emotionally. It is such a personal, subjective matter that there is little or nothing that can or should be said about it.

From this it is assumed that, in the sphere of aesthetic appreciation, reasoning is inappropriate, irrelevant or incoherent. Indeed, it may even be regarded as obtrusive, and destructive of the spontaneity of feeling which is essential to creative artistry, for both performer and spectator. This is a plausible position, since most of us would probably agree that the arts are usually closely concerned with the emotions, and, as we have seen, it is commonly believed that if something is a matter of feeling it cannot be a matter of reason.[1]

Yet this creates the other horn of the dilemma in the form of a very embarrassing consequence, for how can one hold such a view and, consistently, continue to teach dance? Perhaps one can, consistently, be both a subjectivist and a teacher of the *history* of dance. But most teachers of dance do not consider themselves limited to that. On the contrary they usually regard it as more important to try to develop in their students qualities of movement, and an increasing capacity for sensitive appreciation and response. They feel justified in helping their students to eradicate movement of "poor" quality, and they certainly do not feel that any dance, even by a tyro, is as "good" as any other dance. Yet this is precisely the position to which they are committed by an insistence on the subjective status of aesthetic quality in dance. Arnaud Reid (1969) may be right to suggest that there is a link between the prevalence of traditional expressionist

---

[1] Shawn (1946), for example, says that religion is a matter of feeling, not of intellect, as if the terms were mutually exclusive.

theories of art, with their stress on subjective emotional response, and the Cinderella status of the arts in education. If the "teaching" of art consists, for example, of simply giving out the paints and allowing children to express themselves, without guidance at any stage, it is small wonder that the arts are subordinated to subjects of serious study in the curriculum. (I am not, of course, suggesting that there is no place for allowing freedom of expression in the teaching of the arts).

It is difficult to see how, on a subjectivist view, the arts could justifiably lay claim to any role in education beyond that of relaxation or catharsis. If an activity is not rational in any sense, then the notion of standards cannot be applicable to it, since to set a standard necessarily involves the possibility of giving reasons which refer to observable phenomena. And without standards it is hard to see how an activity could be regarded as educational.

The dilemma, then, is that the dance teacher feels it to be not only justifiable, but professionally incumbent on her, to set standards for her pupils. Yet if aesthetic quality is answerable solely to subjective feeling she cannot do this, since it would be an inaccessibly private matter and thus incommunicable.

Before pursuing this further we should, perhaps, dismiss an argument often raised in support of a subjective position, which may persistently cloud the issue, and which goes something like this:

> The impression I have of the dance, whether as performer or spectator, comes through my senses. I cannot perceive the dance through anyone else's sense organs. Therefore my impression is, precisely, *my* impression and no one else's. Therefore the impression I have of the dance is purely subjective

This argument may be plausible, but it won't do, since it would apply equally to such paradigms of objectivity as mathematics and physical objects, as we saw when we considered the case for solipsism in section D (1). It is only by means of my own faculties that I perceive that 2 + 2 = 4, and that the table is brown. Nevertheless such judgments are objective. Hence the objectivity/subjectivity distinction has to come entirely within an acceptance of the platitude that my impression is my impression. There is no support in the obvious fact that I can know nothing about the dance except through my senses for the view that aesthetic response is purely subjective. The trouble is that there is sometimes a temptation to set up an incoherently ideal standard of objectivity which would make it quite independent of human powers of perception.

Of course it might be that someone who supports this subjective argument would agree that it does apply equally to mathematics and physical objects, which would be to argue for general scepticism. It would be like the arguments for solipsism, which, as we saw, limits everything that there is and can be known to what occurs in my own mind, and so effectively denies that there can be any objective judgment. However, it would take us too far afield to discuss that issue in detail, and anyway it does not seem any more necessary now than it did in section D (1). For those who argue in the way outlined are usually making a point specifically about *aesthetic* judgments, i.e. *vis à vis* those in mathematics and about physical objects, which are agreed to be objective.

To return to the difficulties for a subjective view of the aesthetic quality of dance, we can now see them as deriving from the inherent confusion of the traditional dualist view of the emotions, according to which when I feel fear, for example, this is a purely private emotion caused in me by the feared object. The relation is contingent—it just happens to be the case that this object causes this particular inner feeling in me. But, as we have seen, that creates an insuperable problem about how I learn the meaning of an emotion word, for I cannot know that the emotion I feel, which I call "fear," is the same as that felt by others confronted by the same object, and which they call "fear." We cannot compare our feelings since, according to the theory, each person's feeling is entirely private. Worse still, I should be unable even to recognise the same feeling recurring in me on a later occasion, since I have no criterion of sameness if all depends on an inner feeling. Even with the same object there would be no way of knowing whether my feeling about it is the same as I had in similar circumstances on a previous occasion. Hence I could not even know what I am feeling, and all talk of emotions would be impossible.

However, we found in Section E that the relationship between feeling and object is logical, and further corroboration for that contention is provided by considering inappropriate or unreasonable emotional reaction. For it is significant that extreme cases of this sort are regarded as so irrational as to require psychiatric treatment. If, for example, someone were to behave in a way normally characteristic of extreme fear, e.g. paling, sweating, shaking and cowering away, when confronted with a perfectly ordinary currant bun, we should, under normal circumstances, regard his reaction as so incongruous as to raise doubts about his state of mind.

There is a similar limitation on what could be regarded as a normal, reasonable response to a work of art, or artistic performance. We considered in section A the example of *Adagio for a Dead Soldier,* which was clearly an expression of agonised grief. We found that if artistic expression is a matter of inaccessibly private feelings, then this dance could be interpreted as expressing *joie de vivre,* but we should be completely at a loss to understand anyone who responded in this way. Such a reaction would be as abnormal, as irrational, in its own way as that of fear towards a currant bun. The important point is that the feeling, in the sense of an inner, unobservable event, cannot be the criterion of artistic meaning, whether by performer or spectator. If it were, there could be no way of telling whether it was correct or not, since there would be no standard to which to refer it. There would be no distinction between a response's being appropriate and seeming appropriate, no distinction between correct and incorrect interpretation, even broadly. Absolutely any or no feeling would be equally right for any given work—which is to say that the whole notion of artistic expression would be unintelligible. Response to the arts may be emotional, but that is not to say that just *any* feeling would be appropriate, or even comprehensible—as is an inevitable, though not always recognised, consequence of subjective theories of aesthetics.

Of course, where a dance, such as Ballet Rambert's *Blindsight,* is of such complexity that it cannot be categorised simply, even in a broad, undiscriminating way, it may well be that a spectator who is insensitive, or insufficiently experienced in this or any art form, may fail to understand, or may misunderstand it. This would be a misunderstanding which we could understand—for I am certainly not suggesting that there is a correct interpretation or set of responses to every artistic performance. Far from it. But nevertheless there are *limits* to the possibility of correct interpretation. One could not, under normal circumstances, see *Adagio for a Dead Soldier* as a joyful dance, one could not understand it and have *joie de vivre* responses to it.

Interpretative reasoning, we found, does not necessarily lead to definitive conclusions, but that certainly does not imply that in any problem where it is employed any conclusion is as good as any other. A complex work of art may provoke irreconcilable disagreements even among experts, though each may be able to give good reasons for his view of its meaning, but not just any interpretation could intelligibly be proposed. For there is a logical relationship between the work and our interpretation of and feeling about it. So that when we want to know about someone else's aesthetic response we do not attempt to conduct causal inferences to his private, inner, subjective feelings, which, anyway, would make it as incomprehensible as the traditional view makes the emotions generally. To explain one's response to a dance is to give not causes but reasons for a particular way of looking at it, so that the artistic performance under precisely *this* description can be understood as the object of one's feeling. Or, to put the same point in another way, there may be no other possibility of referring to this particular feeling, since "The sadness of the *Adagio*" is not one title among many for it. The sadness is not identifiable *apart* from that dance, which significantly differentiates it from a causal relationship, in which cause and effect are separately identifiable. So that, as in the case of non-aesthetic emotions, to give reasons in favour of an alternative interpretation is to attempt to change the character of the criterial object and therefore of the aesthetic response itself. When we see the dance differently, we feel differently about it. Similarly, if the psychiatrist can convince the patient that this really is just an ordinary currant bun, which, like other ordinary currant buns, is quite harmless and pleasant to eat, his feeling about it will change *pari passu* with his change of view of the object. (This is, of course, to make a gross oversimplification of such cases in order to make the point clearly.)

This is not to deny that many more questions arise about the correctness of one's interpretation of a dance than about the correctness of reaction to a currant bun, and this is true even of a relatively unambiguous example, such as *Adagio for a Dead Soldier*. The difference, which we shall discuss more fully in section F (3), is largely a consequence of that central feature of a work of art, to which any theory of aesthetics must be adequate, namely the indefinite though not unlimited possibility of interpretation. There is far greater complexity in the case of a work of art, but this is a difference of degree, not of kind. It does not affect the issue of principle concerning rational response which is argued here.

It may help to see what is involved in aesthetic appreciation, and the giving of reasons for it, to consider an analogy with chess, in which, for simplicity, a decisive move in chess will be compared with a particularly significant movement in a dance.

The movement of a chess piece is not comprehensible in isolation. We can appreciate its significance only in relation to the situation of the other pieces in that particular game, which itself can be understood and appraised only in the context of what it is to play chess. Some of the individual moves by both players in the sixth game of the recent world chess championship were rapturously acclaimed by the connoisseurs. Obviously the importance of each such move could be appreciated only by taking into account the positions of the other pieces at that precise juncture of the game. And the standard of play of Fischer and Spassky in the game as a whole could be estimated only against a background of many other games of chess, in circumstances where the activity is played and discussed.

Appreciating the significance of a particular tactical move in chess, like appreciation of the arts, is not concerned with causes. It is irrelevant to consider what caused the player's hand to move as it did, what caused the physiological changes in the brain, or what private feelings or thoughts he experienced prior to or concurrently with the move. Understanding and appreciation consists in seeing how importantly it affects the whole network of pietes on the board. The brilliance of a tactical move cannot be explained simply by considering the way in which that particular piece was moved, but by giving reasons which show its relation to, and consequences for, the wider context of the game, and by comparing or contrasting it with tactics in other games of chess, in order to point up its merits. The explanation has to look beyond the move itself to the situation in which it occurs.

Now of course I am not suggesting that appreciation of artistically expressive movement is in every respect, or even in many respects, like appreciating a chess move. The point of the analogy is to bring out something of the character of explaining and comprehending artistic meaning. For it is often supposed that it is something about that particular dance movement which gives it artistic meaning. In this respect there is a sense in which the suggestion made in section B (3), that the emotion is in the movement itself, may be misleading. It may be taken to imply support for the commonly encountered misconception that to discover the artistic meaning of a movement we need to concentrate exclusively on just that movement in order to find what makes it artistic. For example, the question is often asked, among teachers and students of dance and physical education, "What makes a particular movement specifically a *dance* movement?" The difficulty is that, taken by itself, it may be indistinguishable from the same movement performed in gymnastics. Yet one is a dance movement, the other is not. How can we account for the difference? There is a great temptation to think that the answer is to be found in some quality which is intrinsic to the movement itself, and since it cannot be discerned, to conclude that it must be a quality of feeling lying behind the physical action which is the distinguishing feature. But that, of course, leads us back to the confusions of the traditional view. The mistake is to be looking in the wrong direction. To find what endows the movement with artistic meaning, we should be looking not more deeply, but more widely; not at what lies behind, but at what lies around, i.e. at the other movements which precede and follow it, making it part of a pattern without which it would not have that meaning. So to give reasons for the appreciation of a particular movement in a performance is much more like explaining a chess move, it is to try to show its importance, in relation to the other movements, for a particular interpretation of, and therefore an appropriate emotional response to, the dance. The movement is revealed as contributing to, as well as deriving its meaning from, *this* way of looking at the performance, as the criterial object of our feeling about it.

Notice that to give reasons in this way is not necessarily to employ words exclusively. Here again the analogy between chess and dance holds. We could explain why we regard a tactical move in chess as masterly by *showing* someone who is unable to see it, perhaps by setting up the pieces again, the probable consequences of a failure to perform just this move at this juncture. Similarly, a dancer can show how different the response to the performance would have been if an especially significant movement had been omitted or altered. And we can show our understanding of a piece of music by humming it with the appropriate expression, stressing certain phrases in various ways. It is a common experience to feel frustrated in our attempts to describe the non-verbal arts in words, and there is good reason for this as we shall see in section H. Nevertheless, as Wollheim says (1968):

> It almost looks as though in such cases we can compensate for how little we are able to say by how much we are able to do.

Another important similarity between the two cases, which has consequences for justifying the inclusion of the arts in the curriculum, is this. Only someone with a good grasp of chess would be capable of appreciating the significance of an incisive move by a grand master, even when it is explained to him, since the explanation will depend upon his background knowledge of comparable situations. The same is true of dance and the arts generally, with an important qualification to which we shall refer below. The greater one's grasp of the art form, no doubt within a particular convention, the greater the possibility of coming to appreciate the complexity of a certain interpretation. This is not, of course, to say that greater experience in dance automatically confers greater understanding. In this, as in other spheres, sensitivity and aptitude are also required.

The qualification is this. Whereas the justifying reasons which we give for our appreciation of the move in chess rest ultimately on the activity called "playing chess" (its rules, conventions etc.) justifying our appreciation of the dance movement may draw from an indefinitely wide area. Wollheim (1958):

> Art rests on the fact that deep feelings pattern themselves in a coherent way all over life and behaviour.

In giving reasons for the relevance of a certain movement to an interpretation of a dance performance we may be appealing to experiences of life outside art. There is no limitation, as there is in the chess case. To take a somewhat artificially simple example, the reasons given for seeing a dance movement as expressing sadness will ultimately depend on a recognition of its relationship to other expressions of sadness, they will, at least implicitly, reveal similarities and associations with other actions and life-situations which move us emotionally in this way. Sad expressions in art can ultimately be understood as such only by reference to the primary expressions of sadness in life.

Rush Rhees (1969), writing of understanding poetry:

> It is not just the "associations" of the words; it is also the way things are said. You have to know the life to which these remarks and phrases and expressions belong: the force and the importance which they commonly have. I say that the phrases of poetry belong to the same language as ordinary speech (not necessarily that they are *phrases* of ordinary speech). This brings them the depth or the illumination or the forcefulness which they have. "How can one combination of phrases be deeper than another?" Only because those phrases belong to the language and so to the lives of people that will read them.

This is, of course, certainly not to say that meaning in the arts is the same as that in life situations. Rhees asks why anyone should want to study a Turner painting:

> What makes it "like a sunrise" is not that it is a painting *of* a sunrise; for then it would be a poor substitute and it were better to wait for the real thing. . . A work of art belongs to a life and to a culture, and it is important or trivial in that way.

Expressive meaning in the arts, though not the same as, is significantly related to, expressive meaning, mainly in the behaviour of people, in situations outside art. So that, inevitably, a mistaken view of the emotions generally will lead to confusion about what is expressed in art.

We can now see how the insuperable problem for the teaching of the arts arises in the first place. The dilemma presupposes the traditional view of the emotions, with its oversimple dichotomy separating the emotional from the rational. When we recognise that we can give reasons for the way we feel emotionally, the dilemma dissolves. We can consistently both accept the central importance of personal response to the arts, and insist on standards.

F:

REASONS

(3) Reasoning and interpretation

It was suggested in section F (2) that the difference between normal responses to such objects as currant buns and to works of art could be seen as a difference of degree rather than of kind. To support that contention we need to look more closely at other issues which have so far received insufficient attention.

In section E (1), it was said that the notion of the criterion would be used, later in the argument, in a wider sense than that intended by Wittgenstein, who held that if X is a criterion of Y then the presence of X is necessarily a reason for the presence of Y. Thus cold, wet, drop-sensations are criteria of rain, and the criterion for one's knowing the meaning of a word is that one uses it correctly. But we are now using the term, in relation to the emotions and to aesthetic response, in a rather wider sense than that, though it remains a logical relation. People respond differently to the same work of art—indeed the same person may feel differently about the same work of art on different occasions. Though the work sets conventional limits to the feelings which would be appropriate as a response to it, within those limits there may be an indefinitely wide range of variations. And, as we have seen, however sound the reasons we give for a particular interpretation, they do not necessarily lead to universally compelling conclusions. So a criterion, in this sense, cannot necessarily be a reason for a particular interpretation of a work of art.

But to try to draw a sharp distinction between the wide and narrow sense of a criterion would be a misconceived enterprise. There are many distinctions which cannot be rigidly delineated, such as that between the bald man and the man with hair, which are nevertheless useful. It would be odd to insist that the distinction makes sense only if a certain number of hairs can be specified, below which a man should be regarded as bald. Wittgenstein draws attention to what he calls the fluctuation in grammar between criteria and symptoms, i.e. criteria and evidence (1953 § 354). The lodestone is a good illustration of what he means. At one time, presumably, it was discovered by empirical evidence that lodestones attracted iron. No exceptions were found over a considerable period of time, so the correlation became firmly established. Indeed, it became *so* well established that the property of being magnetic became built into the very *concept* of a lodestone, i.e. it became part of the meaning of "lodestone." So that now, if a substance failed to attract iron it could not, as a matter of logic, be a lodestone, any more than a bachelor could be married. Being magnetic, once evidence, is now a criterion for a lodestone.

Similarly, one might say, there is a fluctuation in grammar between criteria in the narrow sense and criteria in the wider sense, though it must be stressed that in either sense a criterion is a matter of *logic*, it depends upon the relevant concept. The behaviour of the road accident victim, in the circumstances of its occurrence, is a criterion of his pain, but the work of art is not a criterion of the emotional response to it in the same sense. For it is only *under a certain description* that a work of art is a criterion of the feeling one has for it. This, perhaps, is what Wittgenstein means by saying that what goes to make the content of emotions "grammatically" different from sensations is that emotions do not give us any information about the external world, (1967 § 491). It may be quite obvious that the man being chased by a bull is afraid, but very often we cannot be sure how to interpret someone's behaviour, or even our own sensations. Within limits there is a range of possible emotional reactions to given circumstances, depending upon how the criterial object is seen. A poor man, winning fifty pounds, may be overjoyed, whereas to a rich man the same win may be a matter of indifference. But if each receives a broken leg in an accident, their respective sensations of pain will not normally vary so widely, even if their attitudes to the injury are different. Nevertheless, there are cases in which hypnotic suggestion, for example, may induce people to see a normally pain-producing situation in a different way, and this may actually reduce or eliminate the pain. Dancers in some primitive tribes reach a trance-like state in which they can walk over burning embers, and perform other such feats without feeling pain. So though there is a difference between the wide and narrow senses of a criterion, it is not a sharp one. There may be a wider range of interpretation in the case of works of art, but if we go beyond certain limits we can be wrong in artistic judgments just as in judgments about physical objects mathematics and science.

We saw earlier, in section F (1), that there is a continuum between simply seeing a certain situation, and interpreting it. Or, to put the same point another way, there is no sharp line between a plain fact and a situation which has been interpreted. The relation of straight perception to interpretation is well illustrated by an example given by Wittgenstein of a drawing which can be seen as a duck or as a rabbit (1953, p 194).[1]

[1] Reproduced by kind permission of Basil Blackwell, Oxford.

Two people, one seeing it as a duck, the other as a rabbit, are seeing the same thing, in the sense of the same configuration of lines. But there is a sense in which each sees something quite different, and could give reasons for seeing it in that way by describing features of the drawing, for example, "There are its ears". These features, seen in this way, contribute to seeing the whole drawing in one particular way, and if that is the only way in which he sees it, it may seem odd to talk of interpreting it. I cannot, for example, see a gnarled tree-trunk *as* a gnarled tree trunk, but I may be able to see it as an ogre. One does not see a camel or a conventional drawing of a camel, as a camel—one simply sees a camel or a drawing of a camel. But Hamlet could point out to Polonius a cloud which could be seen as a camel, a weasel or a whale. Polonius at first sees only a cloud, it is only when Hamlet suggests that interpretation of it that he can see it as a camel. And anyone who could see it in any of the ways suggested by Hamlet would then be able to choose how to see it. But it would not be an unlimited choice, any more than someone who can see the drawing either as a duck or a rabbit has an unlimited choice. He cannot see it as a clock, for instance.

However, it may be that even when a particular interpretation is pointed out to someone he cannot see it. He may be able to see the duck all right, but quite fails to understand how it can be seen as a rabbit. This sort of situation has important consequences for aesthetic appreciation, and the reasons given for it. It partly explains why artistic judgments are so often regarded as merely subjective, since not everyone can see the same thing in a work of art, and therefore why arguments about aesthetic interpretation can become so heated and irreconcilable. For, to return to the simple case, if one person sees only a rabbit, and another only a duck, there is a sense in which they cannot be said to be looking at the same thing. For that would imply that the description given by one could be substituted without change of meaning for the description given by the other. Thus, especially where the interpretation of a situation involves strong moral, religious or artistic convictions, one can begin to see why it may be impossible to reach some sort of neutral description of the facts to which the disputants could refer in order to try to understand each other's views. Consider, to adapt an example of Miss Anscombe's, the case of a tribe which worships the sun as a god. It has, for them, a central significance in a whole interlocking network of religious and moral codes, social practices, artistic tradition and language. On the other hand, to a scientist the sun is simply a mass of burning gas. The term is used as part of a completely different set of concepts. So there is an important sense in which a tribesman and the scientist, both looking at the sun, *cannot* see the same thing, since the criterial object of perception in each case is so very different.

This illustrates how complex are the issues where we have disagreement over the meaning and appreciation of the arts. Even experts may quite literally fail to understand each other's interpretation of the same work of art, since there is an important sense in which they may not be seeing the same thing.

It also allows us to see more clearly the misconception inherent in behaviourism. For whereas a scientist may be able to measure, and give a physical account of, a drawing, and explain physiologically one's perception of it, *that* sort of enterprise will not explain why I see it as a duck instead of a rabbit, since exactly the same scientific explanation would apply to my seeing it as a rabbit. An explanation in terms of physical causes is not on the same plane as one in terms of interpretative reasons. It has a place in a different set of concepts, a different language game, a different way of looking at the situation. So the two types of explanation cannot be interchangeable.

Suppose that someone's foot comes into violent contact with my shin. There is no doubt about the sensation of pain which I experience, and there may be none about the causal explanation of the movement of his leg. But just from this information it is not possible to give an unambiguous account of his *action,* for which an interpretation is required which will both determine and be determined by my attitude towards the incident. It may be that his foot slipped, or he may have intended to kick a ball, and I inadvertently got in the way. It would be inaccurate to describe either eventuality as "He kicked me." On the other hand he may have performed the movement intentionally. So we have three possibilities, in each of which the scientific explanation and the pain-sensation is the same, but in only one of which can I accurately describe what happened as "He kicked me."

There is no single, accurate way of giving the facts about such an incident, which can be obtained by scientific examination. The facts about the *action,* as opposed to the physical movement, depend upon how the incident is seen, i.e. upon one's attitude towards it. And one's attitude is itself determined by assumptions made about the intentions of the person concerned, which involves seeing his behaviour under a certain description. It requires our taking into account not just an isolated physical event but, implicitly, wider factors such as the circumstances in which it occurred, and our knowledge of the person concerned. This illustrates the difference between the two senses of criterion, for, though my interpretation of, and hence my emotional reaction to, his behaviour will vary according to how I see his intentions, my sensation of pain may be unaffected by the way his action is described. He may give me reasons, for example, which convince me that I had misinterpreted the incident, and that his action was not intentional. My resentment is evaporated, but not the pain.

Similarly, someone who cannot appreciate the aesthetic quality of meaning of expressive movement is not on that account suffering from defective eyesight. In this respect ironists themselves sometimes suffer the ironic fate of having their work taken at its face value. But to see such a work of art in this way is to have gone beyond the limits of what could be regarded as correct interpretation. If one fails to notice the subtlety in the writing of Chaucer or Jane Austen, for instance, which makes their work ironical, then one has so far failed to understand it. One's interpretation is incorrect, and one's response inappropriate. Perhaps one needs to have this aspect pointed out, especially if one has not met examples of irony before. Someone more experienced and perceptive may be able to give reasons for seeing the irony in it by picking out features of the work whose significance had been missed. We may then come to see it differently, and thus to feel differently about it. A few subtle nuances, now appreciated, might alter the whole character of the work. They could change one's feeling of indifference or distaste for a portrait seen as sycophantic, to delight at an exquisitely biting satire. The writing has completely changed, it may be impossible henceforth to see it in the way one did before. Yet the words have not changed. A painting by Francis Bacon, seen by someone unacquainted with his work, may seem to be just a pointlessly twisted, distorted face, quite unlike any human being. But when it is explained to him parts of it may take on an altogether different significance and thus change the meaning of the painting as a whole. Yet the painting and canvas remain unaltered, and there has been no change in the perceptive faculties of the spectator. The interpretative reasons have transformed the criterial object, so he sees and reacts to something different.

And however carefully we watch the expressive movements of a dancer we may fail to appreciate just what she is expressing until someone explains it to us. Our attention is drawn to certain shades of phrasing which combine the movements into previously unrecognised patterns, which suffuse the whole performance with a new dimension of meaning. Suddenly it all makes sense—yet, from a purely physical point of view, we now see nothing that was not there before.

Nevertheless there may not be a single correct or genuine interpretation of the dance performance, compared with which others necessarily reveal a lack of artistic insight and understanding. Critics sometimes speak of "the definitive interpretation", by an actor or dancer in a certain role, but it is salutary to remember that no particular interpretation is logically compelling, however obvious *in fact* one may be. A picture of an old man walking up a steep slope, leaning on a stick, might seem to allow for no other interpretation, but it would look just the same if he were sliding downhill in that position. By adding more detail to the picture the practical ambiguity could be reduced, but the theoretical ambiguity cannot be eliminated. It will always be possible for it to be seen in a different way. However, that is certainly not to say that interpretation is an arbitrary matter. An arrow, on a signpost, was not simply chosen at random from other possible symbols. It means "go in this direction" because our way of life is one in which arrows have been generally used, and are known to travel point-first. Similarly, the meaning of an expressive movement in dance derives from, and in its turn contributes to, a whole cultural tradition and the life of a society. So, though a particular movement may be open to various interpretations, this does not imply that we can simply choose any meaning whatever for it. Different cultural traditions may set different limits to the area within which interpretations can be understood as correct, and even within the same society the conventions, and with them the limits of correct interpretation, may change. In this way art, and appreciation of art, are tied to history. Moreover, individual differences of sensitivity and understanding affect the possibility of seeing and responding to the arts. The unperceptive may achieve only a broad, general idea of the meaning of a performance, their understanding may be limited to "It is sad", or "Her lover has been killed." Such promiscuous characterisations are too crude to capture the finer shades of what is being expressed, they are criteria of shallow, limited feelings. Fully to appreciate the arts one needs to have developed the capacity imaginatively to grasp and respond emotionally to complex interpretations.

We found that there is a fundamental sense in which everything, to be understood at all, must be interpreted, must be seen under some description or other. Even in mathematics and science the theories which allow facts to be comprehensible as such are always open to revision. So that what there is, the world itself, is, in this sense, how we see it. Nevertheless, there is a much wider measure of universally accepted basic agreement in these areas than in what are often regarded as "subjective" areas of human experience. If there were disagreement at this underlying level the consequences would be much more far-reaching. Jonathan Bennett (1965), for example, shows that we could not make sense of the notion of someone's being "size blind", i.e. unable to make size discriminations, and to understand our reasons for saying that one object is bigger than another. The ramifications lead to such confusions that the hypothesis can hardly be coherently stated, unlike colour-blindness, which does not radically affect our possibility of understanding each other. It would take us too far afield to discuss this issue in the detail it merits, but it does allow us to appreciate that the difference between the wide and narrow sense of criterion, the difference between perceiving things and interpreting them, the difference between response to such objects as currant buns and response to works of art, are all in fact aspects of the same difference, and that is a matter of degree.

F:

REASONS

(4) Reasoning in aesthetics and morality

In the example given in section F (3) it is clear that it is impossible to understand what "the sun" means to members of the tribe apart from the whole way of life in which the sun plays so central a part. To fail to grasp this is to slip into the definitional fallacy, of thinking of the meaning of a word as something fixed and separable from the language of which it is a part. We saw in section B (2) how tempting it can be to take word-meanings as the basic units, the building bricks from which a whole language is constructed. But this is a fundamental misconception. The meaning of a word or term can be understood only by coming to see the part it plays in the whole language and way of life of the people using it. D.Z. Phillips (1970), for example, argues that philosophers have tended to misconceive the character of religious statements about immortality because of a failure to grasp this point. Such statements have been taken to be answerable to questions such as "How can it make sense to speak of the same man's dying yet coming to life again, or continuing to live, in some sphere which is quite beyond the possibility of our experience?" But this entirely misses their significance.

To understand their meaning we have to look at the part they play in the lives of people who have a religious belief in immortality.

Similar considerations apply to meaning in the arts, in that the reasons we give for appreciation and interpretation of a work of art are ultimately inseparable from the cultural traditions of the community of which they form a part. Aesthetic reasoning, in this respect, can perhaps be most illuminatingly compared with moral reasoning. One can appreciate that some moral views, though different from one's own, are nevertheless moral views. The reasons given for them appeal to ideals, or facts about human welfare, which, though determined by a different moral attitude, can be imaginatively understood. This is why it is, by and large, the educated man who is more able to appreciate an opposing view as a moral view.

We saw in section F (1) that to explain why a certain action was, or ought to be, performed is to reveal to that extent one's moral beliefs, it lays out a way of seeing the situation, perhaps in the hope of commending it to others. A thoroughgoing justification of a moral position will require the unravelling of a whole connecting web of values. The reasons employed draw their content from the underlying attitude of the person giving them, and, to carry any weight, depend upon a measure of shared beliefs in the hearer. One tries to convince someone of the value of an artistic tradition, an approach to art, or an interpretation of a work of art, in a similar way. One draws attention to facets of a different style of music, literature, painting or dance, which might appeal to the aesthetic sensibility of one's audience. Someone whose musical background is exclusively classical may find it difficult or impossible to appreciate Schoenberg. And if the style is sufficiently different, for example John Cage, or some forms of oriental music, he may be unable to accept it as music, as opposed to a formless succession of sounds. Consider, too, the difficulty of comprehension experienced by those who are used to a more perceptual, or representative, approach when they meet modern conceptual painting, with its refusal to give an impression of depth, and its revealing of several perspectives in the same figure. Painters of this genre are concerned to show much more about the subject than can be taken in simply by a visual perception, so they may eschew chiaroscuro and substitute colour for it. Yet without perspective and chiaroscuro, the person who knows only the perceptual has lost the familiar landmarks by which he can understand painting. So that even an early work of Picasso's like "Les Demoiselles d'Avignon" may be difficult to accept.

Similar considerations arise with respect to different styles of dance. Someone who has been absorbed exclusively in the tradition of classical ballet may find it hard to appreciate the work of Martha Graham, Paul Taylor or Alwin Nikolais. And those whose experience is limited to western styles can have only a limited comprehension, at most, of oriental dance, with the precise meanings of particular hand gestures. One may admire the extraordinary dexterity of Ram Gopal, for instance, and the aesthetic (as opposed to artistic) quality of his movements, but without some knowledge of the tradition within which he is working it is impossible adequately to appreciate the artistry of his dancing. In extremely contrasting cases it may be difficult to believe that one is watching dance and not just aimless, unstructured movement or, at the other extreme, emotionally and imaginatively barren formalism. To be able to appreciate reasons given for a different approach to art, as to morality, requires a measure of common background of attitude which gives them point.

Moreover, contrary to popular belief, reasons cannot be used in a neutral sense to decide between conflicting moral standpoints. Moral conclusions cannot be reached from ideally rational, extra-moral arguments, or by reasons which refer to non-evaluative facts about human welfare. The facts, or the significance of facts, about human welfare are already *determined* by a moral attitude, which is therefore a presupposition already written into the justifying reasons. The same is true of aesthetic reasoning. Though apparently platitudinous, it is easily overlooked that one can look at a work of art as such only from an artistically evaluative point of view, and thus reasons for a judgment upon it derive from one's attitude to the arts. There are no non-evaluative facts by reference to which judgments of aesthetic appraisal can be made, whether of a particular work of art or of an artistic tradition. It is significant, for example, that if a critic were to write a purely descriptive account of a concert performance, that would actually imply a depreciatory view of it.

We said that, in contrast to chess, reasons given to support what is said about the meaning of an expressive movement in dance may appeal to experiences outside art. It can now be seen just how far-reaching this appeal may be. We have seen that emotion concepts in art are understandable as such by virtue of their relation with emotion concepts in life outside art, and that the justification of emotional responses may be moral. So clearly there can be no sharp line which can be drawn round the area which is relevant to understanding the arts. To take an obvious example, the nature of art and aesthetic appreciation in a community with strong religious convictions is likely to be very different from that in a community without them. Art grows out of and in turn influences the life of a society. Complex art forms reflect and contribute to a complex civilisation.

> It is not only difficult to describe what appreciation consists in, but impossible. To describe what it consists in, we would have to describe the whole environment. (Wittgenstein, 1966).

This raises one of the peculiar difficulties of considering aesthetics from a philosophical point of view. The concepts of epistemology, such as mind and matter, which are now regarded as central, have always been so regarded, and have remained relatively unchanged through the centuries, so that we are studying the problems which have confronted philosophers since Plato. But art is much more closely tied to particular historical positions. While, at a given period, certain facts may be irrelevant to appreciation of the arts, these same facts may become highly significant at a later period. This is not to say that a detailed knowledge of history is required, but that without some background of socio-historical perspective it is impossible to understand art.

Though artistic judgments can be made only from within the framework of a social and cultural background, this does not imply that no sense can be given to the notion that some traditions may be better than others. One tradition may allow for a greater range of expression of the diverse, subtle feelings and experience which are the province of art. For example, music which employs the variety of tonal qualities in the instruments available to a modern symphony orchestra has a commensurately greater range of expressive possibility than that which is limited to a few primitive instruments. Similarly one tradition of dance may allow for greater diversity of expressive movement than another.

There are two opposite dangers of error here, which are parallel to those concerning interpretation of particular works of art which we considered in section F (3). On the one hand, though there are different artistic traditions, each of which may, from its own point of view, be regarded as allowing for the greatest range and depth of expression, this is not to say what we can simply choose which of them to adopt. On the other hand, though we cannot choose, we are not necessarily restricted to understanding only one tradition, and to appreciating art only from that point of view. (One cannot, that is, choose *in general.* It is, of course, possible to choose a specific meaning for a particular gesture, just as the meaning of a word can be stipulated for a particular purpose. But this possibility, whether in language or in art, depends upon a background of non-collusively acquired meanings.)

What we see in the world is determined by the language we speak, by the concepts and theories which are given with it, though there are different languages and conceptual schemes. What we take to be human good and harm is determined by our underlying moral attitude, though there are different moral attitudes. Similarly, our aesthetic judgments are determined by cultural background and artistic traditions, though there are different cultures and traditions. It is not open to us to select from the various ways of looking at art since one is inevitably considering them from an artistic point of view. There is no sense in the notion of detaching oneself entirely from artistic preconceptions in order to make an appraisal of the respective merits of artistic traditions, but neither are we confined to the cultural outlook in which we are brought up. It is rather that the artistic tradition which we acquire sets limits to how fast and how far we can change, and when changes have been made, the limits, though wider than they were, will be those of the modified attitude. A good illustration of the point is the analogy of a mariner who wants to rebuild his ship in mid-ocean. He can carry out alterations only by depending upon the support of the main structure, so he cannot make radical changes. He cannot scrap the old one and start all over again. Similarly, one can develop, broaden, even progressively bring about extensive changes in one's attitude to the arts, but limits are set by a dependence upon one's underlying attitude while one is modifying it in this way. Just as the mariner cannot get off his ship to rebuild it, so it is impossible to adopt an ideally objective, value-independent point of view from which to appraise the relative merits of artistic traditions. The notion is incoherent, since such appraisal presupposes reference to artistic values.

It is possible to come to appreciate the music of a different culture sufficiently to recognise that it is music and not just a jumble of sounds only if there is some overlap between it and what comes within the sphere of one's musical under-standing. This toe-hold allows for the progressive achieve-ment of a more complete comprehension of a very different artistic tradition. So the possibility of a developing apprecia-tion of the arts is not logically unlimited. It is not simply a matter of preference, of simply choosing any interpretation of a work of art.

Another way of putting this point is to say that not *any* reason can be understood as supporting an artistic judgment. The artist gives a perceptive portrayal of the world as it is, which can only be how he sees it. Through the medium of his art he sheds light on details of aspects of our lives the significance of which had escaped our notice.[1] And the critic suggests the way in which art should be seen. The innovators, whether artists or critics, are extending the boundaries of the concept of art within which our judgments are at present confined. Again one is struck by the similarity of grasping the significance of reasons proposed for a new scientific theory, for this makes equally exacting demands on the imaginative powers, on the ability to be open-minded. Think of the enormous effort of conceptual imagination which must have been required to see the world as spherical instead of flat, and how very understandable was the reaction of those who found it so difficult to accept what Copernicus said about the earth's going round the sun, after centuries of belief in the earth as the centre of the universe. This belief was built into the very language, with expressions we still use, such as those about the rising and setting of the sun. To change it so radically necessitated a considerable readjustment of religious, scientific and other interlocking patterns of thought. So that in science, too, what there is depends upon how we see it.

It might be objected that this is not true since now, at any rate, we do know, in an absolute sense, that such people were wrong and Copernicus was right, since it is an indisputable *fact* that the earth goes round the sun. But this misses the point. For, before Copernicus, it was equally indisputable that the sun went round the earth—any serious denial of this "fact" was inconceivable. Scientists were so locked within a theoretical, conceptual system that they could no more consider an alternative than I can see through someone else's eyes. And similarly we are now operating within a different set of theories and concepts which do not allow us to

---

[1] R.W. Beardsmore (1971) gives some good examples of how art can illuminate a moral issue. A different example is Mike Leigh's recent film "Bleak Moments", which perceptively reveals the distortingly rigid limitations set to human relationships by crippling shyness and emotional repression. The film does this by tracing out what this sort of situation *amounts to* in the detailed moments of everyday lives.

conceive of the possibility of a comparably immense change of view in the future.

Such considerations should give pause to those, in the arts as well as in the sciences, who demand or oppose neat, sharp, definitively correct answers, and who too easily dismiss alternative views, or an inability to reach a decisive conclusion, as indicative of ignorance, insensitivity or lack of aptitude. It can also be seen just how important is the role of interpretative reasoning in the arts as in the sciences in revealing new ways of seeing the world.

G:

KINAESTHETIC
EMPATHY

There is another theory of aesthetic meaning which is sometimes proposed, particularly in relation to dance, although analogous versions are applied to the other arts. It is said that aesthetic meaning does ultimately depend upon feeling, but not so much emotional as kinaesthetic feeling, i.e. the feeling of the movement. It will be found that, as it is most commonly interpreted, it is a variant of the traditional view, though it is worth examining in its own right, partly because it is so commonly held, and partly because of some important related issues to which it frequently leads. The thesis is stated in some such way as this:

> The only way to understand dance is to dance. Only by actually experiencing what it feels like to move in the requisite way can one discover the real meaning of what is being expressed. No amount of study and thought can give what one hour's sweat in a studio can give, since appreciation of the aesthetic quality of dance is in the physical experience of the movements. Talking, reading or writing about it can never lead to comprehension of the art of dance—only learning to perform can do that.

It is usually unclear whether the claim is that the performer is necessarily the only person who can understand the dance, or that the performer is necessarily better placed to understand it. But in either case the argument is riddled with difficulties. For instance, those who argue in this way usually also insist that dance is communication. Without pausing to unravel the ambiguities in that statement, we can agree that it implies at least that dance normally has a meaning which can be transmitted from performer to spectator, but this, in conjunction with the thesis above, is a plain self-contradiction. For, to take it in extreme form, if only the particular dancer of each particular dance can understand its meaning, then no one else, not even another dancer, can understand it, in which case there can be no communication.

Even if a weaker version is proposed which would allow that the expressive meaning of dance can be transmitted only to those who have performed similar movements, there are insuperable problems. For this would be comparable to saying that only violinists can understand violin music, which is surely implausible. But there is worse to come, for, on a parallel argument, in order to be able to understand orchestral music one would have to know not only how to play each instrument in the orchestra, but how to play them all at the same time. Very often a member of the audience is in a better position to appreciate orchestral music than any of the players. And if, for instance, he has read a lot about music, has a large, well chosen record library, frequently goes to concerts and listens to music on the radio, someone who cannot play a note may be in a far better position to understand and appreciate music than even an expert performer who lacks such knowledge. A similar position obtains in dance and the other arts. It is most obvious where a performance includes several dancers. A knowledgeable observer is usually in a better position to judge its artistic merit than any of those taking part. But the same considerations apply even to a solo dance, since the spectator can see the whole pattern of movement. This is why dancers and actors usually need producers and directors. Non-performers who are nevertheless connoisseurs of the arts are by no means uncommon.

However, despite these difficulties, there is a tendency among those imbued with the thesis outlined above to feel dissatisfied with the arguments against it, and to insist that there is this ineliminably subjective element about the aesthetic meaning of dance. "For how," a dancer may object, "can anyone else know how it feels to have *this* kinaesthetic sensation? Only I, who have performed the movement, can know how it feels."

Though this is a natural reaction, it can be shown to be either incoherent or false. The most likely sense of the objection reveals how deeply ingrained is the traditional view. It implies that the sensation can be regarded as distinct from the movement, in which case the objection reduces to nonsense. For in that case it should be possible to refer to the sensation without reference to the movement, and how could that be done? To put the point another way, the dancer who says of the sensation, "It feels like *this*", as she performs the movement, has no way of distinguishing between the "it" and the "this." The "it" cannot be specified apart from the "this", the sensation cannot be identified except by the movement. The objection reveals a failure to understand that the movement is not a sign, but a *criterion* (in the narrow sense), of the sensation. To try to refer to the sensation apart from the movement is to try to refer to a something about which nothing can be said.

On the other hand, if it is accepted that the movement and the sensation are inseparable, i.e. that the movement is a criterion of the sensation, then the objection is false. For in that case we are all in principle capable of discovering what it is like to feel that sensation since we can perform, or imagine, similar movements and therefore experience, or imagine what it feels like to experience, similar kinaesthetic sensations.

A further disconcerting consequence of the original thesis is that performances would be comprehensible only to other dancers who have themselves executed exactly similar movements, and thus know what it is like to experience the relevant sensations. That would severely limit audiences.

However, those inclined to this view who come to realise what it entails are usually ready to concede the unacceptability of a theory of aesthetic meaning which denies the possibility of the audience's understanding what is being expressed. So a correlative thesis is proposed in terms of the feelings caused in spectators or in other performers by the dancer's movements:

> The dancer experiences certain kinaesthetic sensations as she moves, and these constitute the aesthetic meaning of the dance. Communication of this meaning is effected by a feeling of empathy in the spectators, caused by watching the performer's movements. Their own bodies thus experience kinaesthetic sensations similar to those of the dancer, and they can understand what she is feeling. This explains how it is that those who have learned how to dance are better able to appreciate its aesthetic meaning than those without such training. Nevertheless, even without direct experience of the movements specific to dance, if one has learned how to move in other ways, for example in gymnastics or games, one is more likely to be able to understand artistically expressive movement than are those whose experience of any sort of physical movement is very limited. It is a matter of degree. Most people, even those with little experience, have some capacity for movement, hence, when watching, they are aware to some extent of what the dancer is feeling. And those with a rich experience, and who are particularly susceptible to this empathy, may feel the kinaesthetic sensations so strongly as to have an almost irresistible urge to dance themselves.

There are variations of the argument, but this seems to be the main tenor of most of them. The aesthetic meaning of a movement is a matter of the kinaesthetic sensations of the performer which are communicated by causing empathetic feeling in the spectator. Causal theories of this kind, though not related specifically to kinaesthetic sensations, are sometimes proposed with respect to the other arts.

This notion of identifying the meaning of dance with

kinaesthetic sensations is analogous to a theory of linguistic meaning which is still very prevalent, and which is notably exemplified by the philosopher John Locke (1961). Locke says that words stand for nothing "but the ideas in the mind of him that uses them." For every meaningful word there is a thought or idea to which it refers. We are not always conscious of the ideas behind our words because we become so familiar with them that we do not always bother to check that they are still backed by the appropriate correlation. Nevertheless, for a verbal expression to be meaningful, it must be possible to call to mind the relevant idea. Failing this, words are "nothing but so much insignificant noise." Communication is possible because when I speak my words excite in other men the same ideas. If a man has not learned to associate words with the correct ideas he cannot be said to understand the language.

It can be seen how similar this Lockean view of language meaning is to the theory that aesthetic meaning in dance is a matter of kinaesthetic sensations. In the same way it is held that a movement has aesthetic meaning only if it is backed by the relevant sensation, and a dancer communicates by exciting corresponding kinaesthetic sensations in her audience, who thereby understand what she is expressing. Just as language is understood only by people who have learned to associate words with the appropriate ideas, so the aesthetic meanings of movements are understood only by those who know what it is like to feel the appropriate sensations while moving. This explains how it is that those whose experience of kinaesthetic sensations is greatest, such as dancers and others who perform varied physical movements, have the greatest comprehension of aesthetically expressive movement in dance. Similarly, greater experience in using language tends to confer greater understanding of word-meanings since it gives more practice at finding the correct words for one's ideas.

These theories are certainly plausible. There is more to word-meaning than just uttering or hearing sounds. There is a difference between making a sound, and making the same sound as a word with meaning. A parrot can be taught to speak a word, but it cannot speak with meaning. It is tempting to suppose that the difference, when the word is spoken with meaning by a language-user, is explained by the concomitance of an idea in the mind of the speaker. Further support seems to come from considering those occasions on which one hears a speaker's words but either misunderstands them or understands nothing by them. Such cases seem to indicate a failure to associate the sounds heard with the appropriate ideas.

The kinaesthetic empathy theory of communicating the aesthetic meaning of dance is equally plausible. There is a difference between simply moving, and performing the same movement with aesthetic meaning. People can be taught to move in certain ways, yet they move without understanding. It is easy to suppose that the difference, when the movement is performed with aesthetic meaning, consists in the concomitance of the correct kinaesthetic sensation. And, analogously, support seems to come from seeing an expressive movement and either misunderstanding it, or understanding nothing by it. Such cases seem to indicate a failure of appropriate kinaesthetic empathy.

A further claim is that the theory of understanding aesthetic meaning through kinaesthetic empathy can overcome the objection raised earlier that this would be like saying that only performers can appreciate the meaning of music. For whereas everyone moves, not everyone plays or listens to music. Hence, it is argued, kinaesthetic empathy, and with it the possibility of comprehending aesthetic meaning in dance, is, to a greater or lesser degree, universal. So that one sometimes even hears it claimed both that this puts dance in a superior position to the other arts, and that physical movement is a universal language which communicates better than verbal language, since everyone moves, but not everyone speaks the same language.

The theory, in any of its forms, depends upon a causal relationship between the dancer's movements and the empathetic sensations excited by them in the spectator. Now

certainly there can be causal connections between movements and sensations, as there can between words and ideas
or sensations. This is exemplified by the psychologist's
word-association tests. The word "dentist", for instance,
might well be associated with, and therefore cause, an
unpleasant sensation in the pit of the stomach. And in a
similar way certain physical movements might be associated
with sensations. But it is important to notice that, whether
for words or for movement, mere concurrence of idea or
sensation is inadequate as an explanation of meaning.
Laurence Sterne makes the point rather neatly in *Tristram
Shandy:*

> "My young master in London is dead!" said Obadiah.
> A green satin night-gown of my mother's which had been twice
> scoured, was the first idea which Obadiah's exclamation brought
> into Susannah's head. Well might Locke write a chapter on the
> imperfection of words.

It is obvious that "My young master in London is dead",
does not mean "A green satin nightgown which had been
twice scoured." Yet on Locke's theory, since that was the
idea which was caused by Obadiah's statement, that must
have been its meaning.

Similarly, it is not enough to explain the meaning of
expressive movement as the sensation a dancer has while
moving, since she could experience any of an indefinite range
of sensations. She might just happen to have an itching
sensation whenever she performs a particular movement, but
obviously that is not its meaning. And the same applies to the
sensations experienced by spectators. The theory is open to
objections similar to those we raised against the traditional
view of the emotions. If the meaning of the movement
depended uniquely upon a causal connection with a sensation, there could be no way of knowing what it was. The
spectator could not tell whether his kinaesthetic sensation
corresponded with that of the dancer.

So despite the additional refinement, to insist that

understanding dance is a matter of kinaesthetic sensations caused by the dancer, is, in this sphere, to make the notion of understanding incoherent, and with it the possibility of aesthetic meaning. For it is unintelligible to allow a contingent connection between word and linguistic meaning, or between expressive movement and aesthetic meaning.

This is not to deny that the dancer may experience characteristic sensations as she moves, or that a spectator may be able to imagine what it feels like to move in that way. But even if we fully accept the consequences of the criterial relation between movement and kinaesthetic sensation, so that it can be said that the spectator can know which sensation the dancer is feeling, this will not do as an account of the aesthetic meaning of the movement. For precisely the same movement, and therefore kinaesthetic sensation, may occur in tennis, skiing, gymnastics or throwing javelins. Considering simply the movement, and corresponding kinaesthetic sensation, in this way, will not give us the aesthetic meaning—for that we need to look at the wider aspect of the context in which the movement occurs.

The point is that kinaesthetic sensations, or any other sensations, cannot be identified with aesthetic meaning, and questions concerning what brought them about belong to the psychology of aesthetics. Thus a psychologist might discover that there are physical changes, and associated sensations, in those who watch or perform certain dances, and from these data he might derive valuable information about the causal effects of dance. But such information is irrelevant to artistic appreciation, since understanding aesthetic meaning is not the same thing as understanding the causal effects of art. If it were, then presumably it would, in principle, be possible for a scientist to develop drugs, electrical apparatus, or something of the sort, which could be substituted for appreciation of art, by giving the same effects. So an interest in the aesthetic meaning of dance is not an interest in the causes of kinaesthetic sensations. It is a matter of interpretation, achieved not by causal investigation, but by seeing the significance of certain aspects of the dance which suggest convincing descriptions of it, and which relate it, implicitly or explicitly, to other emotional expressions both within and outside art.

In the same way, appreciation of chess is not a question of causes and sensations. It would make no difference to an evaluation of the standard of their play to discover that Fischer and Spassky experience certain characteristic sensations during the game. This might be of interest to a psychologist, but it is irrelevant to an appraisal of the quality of chess.

Word-meanings are not a matter of causes either. It may have some Freudian significance that whenever Alan hears the word "tent" it causes certain sensations associated with sexual desire. Nevertheless, when he uses the word "tent" it does not mean "sensations associated with sexual desire." Words may have associations, but those associations are not what the words mean. Equally, what causes one to utter a word is not relevant to its meaning. If it were discovered that tapping people on the left elbow caused them to utter the word "hassle", that would not help us to find out what the word means. Whether of a word, or of an expressive movement, meaning cannot be that with which it just happens to coincide. Meaning demands a context, so to look for it in the ideas or sensations of the speaker or performer is to be looking in the wrong direction. Even if there are sensations which characteristically accompany the performance or observation of a particular type of movement, they are not its meaning, any more than the sinking feeling one might associate with "dentist" is the meaning of that word. If a dancer performed an obviously inappropriate movement we should not be prepared to withdraw an unfavourable evaluation of it on her assurance that, whatever the movement looked like, she experienced the right sensation. Similarly, if someone says something quite inappropriate about a dance performance, our conviction of his lack of comprehension is not going to be modified by what he tells us about his kinaesthetic empathy.

To repeat the point, I am not, of course, denying that

dancers and spectators may experience intense sensations. Some people are greatly affected emotionally by the arts, and, as we saw in section E (2), sensations and bodily changes are characteristic of some emotions. But whatever the sensations, in performer or observer, it is the context of the movement which is all-important for interpreting its aesthetic meaning, and therefore for our emotional response to it. In the same way, an arrow on a signpost does not mean "go in this direction" as a consequence of the sensations one might associate with arrows.

There is a logical relationship between words and their meanings, and between expressive movements and what they mean or express. To analyse the meaning of a verbal expression we trace out its consequences in the various instances of its use. We try to map out its logical geography in the network of language, its relationship to other verbal expressions. Similarly, to discover the aesthetic meaning of an expressive movement is to see its significance in the context of the whole dance. The meaning of a dance is not an aggregate of sensations. It is rather that the individual movements and phrases contribute to a way of seeing the whole dance, and that interpretation in turn endows them with meaning.

To return to the original thesis, we can now see that the dancer is not necessarily better placed to appreciate the aesthetic meaning of her performance than the spectators. It may be true that no amount of reading and thinking can give what one hour's sweat in a studio can give. It is equally true that no amount of sweat in a studio can give what one hour's reading and thinking can give. But, more importantly, this way of looking at the matter is misleading anyway. It implies an incoherent dichotomy between performing dance and thinking about dance. An expert dancer does not merely carry out thoughtless physical movements—rather like reflex actions. She has usually read, talked, and thought a lot about her art generally, and specifically she thinks a good deal about precisely how to perform this particular dance. Her performance is a thoughtful performance.

This is not to say that there is no difference between the dancer and the spectator. Obviously there is. The dancer dances and the spectator watches. But this difference, with a qualification to be mentioned below, is not relevant to the possibility of understanding the aesthetic meaning of the performance. There is a difference between speaking a word and listening to it, but this does not affect the ability to understand its meaning. There is a common, but misguided tendency to give too much weight to what an artist himself says about his work. When the work of art has been produced the artist is, in principle, in no better a position for understanding it than anyone else. Analogously, as we have seen, the person who is experiencing an emotion may be a worse judge of its character than other people.

What the artist says has no greater authority, for example, than the views of perceptive, knowledgeable critics. There is no reason why someone crippled since birth, and therefore unable to dance, should not become expert in the appreciation of artistically expressive movement. If he had read and thought a lot about it, and watched many performances, he might be more able to appreciate it than a first-class dancer who had not considered her art so carefully. It is worth remembering that imagination is required not only to create but also to interpret a work of art.

On the other hand, the artist has no less authority than others, and since he has a peculiarly intimate connection with his work it is usually of considerable interest to listen to what he says about it. But this is not necessarily definitive with respect to its meaning. We might want to reject his account. He may be too close to his work to be able adequately to pass judgment on it.

There is at least one difference between linguistic and aesthetic meaning of which we should be aware, which is largely a consequence of the indefinite possibility of interpretation which is a feature of the concept of a work of art. There is a greater degree of tolerance of correct aesthetic meaning than of correct linguistic meaning, i.e. there are more ways of correctly interpreting aesthetic than linguistic meaning. Nevertheless, this by no means gives a significant advantage, in the comprehension of aesthetic meaning, to the artist. Wollheim (1968) makes the point that for it to be in any way in order to talk of understanding apropos of art, there must be some kind of correspondence between the artist's activity and the spectator's reaction, though in the domain of art the correspondence will never be complete.

> The spectator will always understand more than the artist intended, and the artist will always have intended more than any single spectator understands.

So the difference, though important, is not importantly relevant to the present point, which is that meaning in the arts is neither limited to, nor even necessarily better understood by, the artist. Specifically, the notion that only the dancer can appreciate the aesthetic meaning of dance is a myth, if a somewhat persistent myth, which does the art of dance a disservice.

H:

DANCE AND EMOTIONAL DEVELOPMENT

(1) Feeling and medium

We are now in a position to consider an issue which is related to what is often called the problem of form and content, and which is of some significance for the role of the arts in education.

It is sometimes thought that any of the arts can contribute equally to emotional development. A corollary of this view, more often implied than stated explicitly, is that, strictly, we need to introduce only one of the arts into our institutions of education in order to allow fully for the emotional release, experience or propensity, through aesthetics, of students. What is, in fact, the same conception is often expressed in terms of transfer. It is said, for instance, that if one learns to create and appreciate expressive qualities in dance, it follows that one can subsequently apply what one has learned to music, literature and painting. The notion lying behind this view seems to be that there are certain capacities or states which we call emotions and which can be expressed through, and developed by various artistic media. Having developed one's emotional capacity through the medium of one art form, it is thought that one can then transfer the feeling and sensitivity thus acquired to other art forms.

But this thesis, though plausible and currently popular in some quarters, can be shown to be unintelligible. Examination of it will reveal that it, too, presupposes the traditional view of the emotions. We shall find that, on the contrary, each art form is unique, in the sense that its contribution to emotional development cannot be made by any other art form.

Our rejection of the causal theory of kinaesthetic sensations as an adequate explanation of aesthetic meaning in dance may still leave the dancer, or teacher of dance, dissatisfied. She may still feel that the aesthetic meaning of dance is unique in a way which derives precisely from the fact that the medium of the art is the movement of the human body, and in this she is right. As we have found, traditional theories of the emotions left a logical gap between inner feelings and outer behaviour. Partly as a consequence of this, aesthetic theories tended to err towards one of two extremes. Roughly, they equated the meaning of a work of art either with the subjective state of the artist who created it, or with the physical object he had created. The former extreme, expressionism, lays emphasis on the emotional content of the work, and this has usually seemed to lead inexorably towards an account of aesthetic meaning which depends upon an introspective report by the artist. There appears to be no other way to discover the character of the emotion which is expressed in his art. Thus, on this view, to understand and appreciate the meaning of a dance, it is necessary to know the inner emotional state of the dancer and/or choreographer who created it as an expression of that state.

The latter extreme, which I shall call formalism, stresses the physical form, or medium, in which the work of art is created. (It should be said that not all who call themselves formalists would agree that the forms in which they are interested are exclusively physical aspects of the artefact. But it is convenient at this stage of the argument to focus on an extreme form of the view). Formalists recognise, correctly, that on an expressionist view it would be impossible to understand art. Frequently spectators do not have the opportunity to discover what the artist was feeling as he created his work. Moreover, as we have seen, if a gap were allowed between the emotional content and the physical form, not even the artist himself could know which emotion this work of art is expressing, since he might make a mistake in identifying it. Hence the formalist tends to concentrate on the physical artefact. In this respect he is in a similar position to the behaviourist, who rejects the notion of mental experience because there is no evidence of it. The formalist overcomes the problem of the gap between form and emotional content by the simple expedient of denying that there is any emótional content.

But it is, to say the least, implausible to deny that the arts can be emotionally expressive, for this is a common experience among those of us with artistic interest. Nevertheless, the formalist undoubtedly has a point. It is incoherent to suppose that, in order to discover the meaning of a work of art, we need to delve into the inner recesses of the artist's mind.

It can, perhaps, already be seen that the dispute between the expressionist and the formalist arises from an underlying and unquestioned acceptance by both of the traditional view of the emotions. Both share the assumption that if aesthetic meaning is emotionally expressive, then it is subjective and can be elucidated only by an introspective report by the artist.

Expressionist: The meaning of art consists in the expression of emotions; emotions are subjective, therefore aesthetic meaning is subjective.

Formalist: If the meaning of art consists in the expression of emotions this is tantamount to an admission that art has no meaning. For emotions are subjective, and on a subjective view, aesthetic meaning would be irrational. Since art does have meaning, it cannot be emotionally expressive.

The shared premiss is that if something expresses

emotions, its meaning is subjective and non-rational. And this *is* the traditional theory, with its unintelligible insistence that an emotion is private and accessible only to the person feeling it. We have already exposed mortal flaws in this theory in relation both to emotions generally and to aesthetics in particular. We found that behaviour directed on to an object is a criterion of an emotion, and that a work of art under a particular description is a criterion of what it expresses. These criteria are publicly observable, so the shared premiss is false and the dispute dissolves. Art can be both emotionally expressive and answerable to observable criteria. The error exemplified in this sort of dispute is pervasive. It is revealed in such statements as, "Art is feeling objectified," at least under one interpretation.[1] If to be objectified is to be made perceptible to the senses, then feelings in general already are objectified. Feelings expressed in art are no more and no less objectified than any other feelings.

A way of approaching the problem which is conducive to error from the very formulation of the question is to ask how it is that feelings get into a work of art. For the work is a physical phenomenon, as is physical behaviour, and each is criterially related to the feeling it expresses. So there is as much, or as little, of a problem about how feelings get into sobbing behaviour as there is about how feelings get into a work of art. (There is, of course, a further problem, to which we shall refer later, of how emotions which are normally attributable to living beings can also be said to be in inanimate objects. See Wollheim (1968) for a detailed treatment of this problem). An emotionally moving work of art is not evidence of a feeling. One recognises, by observable features of the work itself, the character of the emotion it expresses. It is that sort of work of art, just as sobbing is that sort of behaviour.

It may help to illuminate this point to compare again

---

[1] Suzanne Langer, for example, says (1957), "The arts objectify subjective reality." And Margaret H'Doubler (1957), "The value of art discipline, a formative process, lies in the ability to objectify emotion."

Locke's theory of meaning in language, according to which thoughts are ideas in the mind for which we find appropriate linguistic labels. Thus, for Locke, a meaningful statement consists of two components. There is the content, or thought itself, as one component, and there is a structural component, which is the linguistic term in which it is expressed. Words are, as it were, the wrappings in which thoughts are delivered. On this view it is possible to have thoughts which are not expressible. But, despite its plausibility, this is an unintelligible thesis. It is true that the meaning of a proposition is not the same as any particular form of words which is used to express it—the meaning of "I have a cat" can be equally well rendered by "J ai un chat." Furthermore, it is certainly a contingent matter that the sentence "I have a cat" expresses the proposition that I have a cat (i.e. has the meaning that I have a cat), since other words might have been used to express that proposition if the linguistic conventions had developed differently. But it is not a contingent matter that the proposition is expressed linguistically in some way or other. Meaning cannot coherently be regarded as independent of any form of expression whatsoever.

This is not to suggest that one has to say what one thinks, or that silent contemplation which does not issue into some form of external expression is impossible. Obviously this often happens. It is to say that no sense can be given to the idea of thinking, even silently to oneself, without a medium in which such thoughts could be expressed. There is no way in which the meaning of a sentence could be identified apart from some externally expressible physical form. To try to do so is to try to talk about a something about which nothing can be said. Thoughts are inseparable from the linguistic forms which are used to express them, though they may be distinguishable if, for instance, one wants to discuss grammatical structure, or decide on the most effective of several synonyms. There is a logical relationship between words and their meanings, between linguistic expressions and thoughts. So in learning a language a child is learning to think.

To relate this to aesthetic meaning, the only answer to the

question "What is expressed in the dance?" which both allows for emotional qualities and does not degenerate into the incoherence of the traditional view, is an answer which points to the dance itself. The emotion expressed in the dance must be inseparable from the physical movement which is the medium peculiar to the art of dance.

However, a significant difference between linguistic and aesthetic meaning is that whereas synonyms may occur in language they are impossible in the arts. To begin to understand why this is so, we need to consider the differences between emotions with respect to their particularity. Emotions can be seen as forming a spectrum, from the rather general, relatively undifferentiated feelings such as anger, joy and depression, at one extreme, to the highly complex and particularised feelings, among which are those characteristically expressed in the arts, at the other extreme.[1] Feelings at the former extreme may be expressed in a number of different ways. For example, there are various behaviour patterns, including what he says, which show that a person is sad—he may walk dejectedly, weep, sigh frequently, remain unwontedly silent, decline to eat etc., and any of these actions would reveal his sadness. So that to say someone is sad is to give a broad characterisation of what he is feeling, since there are several criteria of sadness in general.

As the feelings become more particularised, towards the centre of the spectrum, there is less possibility of expressing each in different ways. Fear of snakes would come into this category, for though there are various ways of expressing such a fear. the possibility is considerably more limited than it is in the case of sadness or fear in general.

At the other end of the spectrum are those highly particularised emotions each of which can be expressed, and specified, in only one way. That is, there is only one criterion for such a feeling, so that apart from *this particular* expression of it, it cannot intelligibly be said to exist. To speak of the sadness of Mozart's Fortieth Symphony is to

[1] See R.W. Hepburn (1965) for a discussion of this notion.

speak of an emotion which could be expressed in no other way. This is the logical rationale underlying the strictures against the so-called "heresy of paraphrase." To change the *form* of expression, whether within the same medium of art, or into a different one, would be to change the criterial object of the emotion, and therefore the emotion itself.

Perhaps the statement, "Music expresses the inexpressible", and Stravinsky's, "Music by its very nature is incapable of expressing anything," though apparently contradictory, are in fact making the same point, namely that it is impossible to express in any other way, for example verbally, what is expressed in music.

Now we can see how this relates to the question of the unique contribution of each art form to emotional development. For these considerations suggest not only that the emotion expressed in each dance, for example, is particular to that physical manifestation, but also that each art form expresses emotions which are particular to it. So in exploring and learning new forms of expression, we are learning new forms of feeling, and thereby gaining and refining the capacity for experiencing new feelings. By presenting to students the possibility of expressing emotion in the medium of physical movement peculiar to dance, the teacher is encouraging them to develop emotions which could not be known in any other way. Thus learning to dance can be a discovery of both formal and emotional qualities. Only through the physical movement which is the medium of dance can one acquire the possibility of expressing those emotions. The opportunity to experience such feelings depends upon the acquisition of an understanding of the expressive movements which are uniquely the province of dance. This is the sense in which each of the arts can contribute uniquely to emotional development. As one increasingly comes to understand an art form, one learns to discern more and more complex interpretations, and therefore to experience more and more complex feelings in response to them. And to give reasons for one's feeling about a complex work of art is a commensurately complicated matter.

This exposes the incoherence of the view that each person has a capacity for aesthetic feeling which can be enriched and enlarged by any art form. Such a view mistakenly conceives of aesthetic sensitivity or creativity as a general state which can be developed by exercise in the various art forms just as muscular strength can be developed by means of various physical activities. But the criteria for aesthetic feeling and response are particular to each art form, and since the emotions are inseparable from the medium in which they are expressed, only those who have learned to understand the medium can experience them. Thus the idea of transfer makes no sense. An emotion expressed in dance is inextricable from the physical movement which is the medium of the art form, so it could not be expressed or felt in music. There would be no way of identifying it. We cannot coherently talk of the possibility of expressing Mozart's Fortieth Symphony in poetry, or of having exactly the same feeling about both it and a poem.

So we can appreciate that the dancer is justified in inisisting that the expressive meaning of dance is uniquely related to the physical movement in which it is expressed. We can also understand why it is that we are so often frustrated in our attempts to describe the non-verbal arts in words, or the verbal arts in other words. The criterial object is given by the work of art in its particular form. No sense can be made of a comprehensive account of the aesthetic content of a dance in another medium, for example in words, since to change the medium is to change the criterial object and therefore the feeling for it. So the same emotion cannot be expressed in both dance and words.

I am not suggesting, of course, that there is nothing which can be said, but rather that not everything can be said about dance in words.

H:

DANCE AND EMOTIONAL DEVELOPMENT

(2) Feeling and medium (continued)

It might help to clarify the issues raised in the foregoing argument to consider three objections which are likely to be raised against it. For simplicity I shall consider them in relation to the teaching of dance to children.

(1) How do we know that children who are learning a particular dance are all learning to experience the same emotion?

(2) How do we know that the feeling expressed in a particular dance is not the same as that expressed in, for example, a piece of music?

(3) How do we know that children are feeling *anything* while dancing?

The first two objections reveal a presupposition of the traditional view, in which there is a logical gap between the emotion and the expression of it. If we allow that, then, as we have discovered, there can be no criterion for the sameness of an emotion, since it becomes inaccessibly private and unrecognisable even by the person feeling it. And that makes it unintelligible to talk of "the same emotion." The feeling is identified by the form of expression, so a different form is a criterion of a different feeling.

Thus the first objection can be overcome by recognising that to know whether children are feeling the same emotions we have to take into account their whole behaviour patterns while dancing. These will be, if not at first the only criteria, the principal criteria for the feeling concerned.

There is a great danger of being misled here by implicitly demanding an inappropriate standard of sameness. The criteria for being the same X depend upon what X is. The notion of identity cannot coherently be considered in general or *in vacuo,* but only in relation to something or other. Differences are still consistent with sameness if those differences are characteristic of that type of thing, since the concept of identity allows for changes within limits. One speaks of the same bicycle, though it now has different handlebars, and of the same tree even though it is now much bigger than when it was last seen as a sapling, and despite the transformation in its appearance as the seasons change. A man might play in the same football team as that in which his grandfather played fifty years ago, though not one player from those days is still playing in it. Indeed, the *lack* of change, in some cases, would count against the claim to identity. A schoolmaster meeting a former pupil whom he has not seen for twenty years, would know that it could not be the same person if the latter's schoolboy appearance remained unchanged.

We do not need to go any further into the difficult philosophical problem of identity. It is enough for our purposes to recognise that one dancer need not be performing physical movements which are indistinguishable from those of another dancer in order to be said to be expressing the same feeling, any more than each person needs to be weeping in order to be expressing the same emotion, of sadness. There will, however, be less scope for difference of expression with respect to the same dance, unless the "life" sadness is highly particularised. So, bearing this in mind, we know that children are learning to experience the same emotion because it can be seen that they are learning the same form of expression, which is criterially related to the feeling being expressed.

The second objection is based upon the same misconception. If the form of expression in a particular medium is the only criterion for the emotion which is being expressed, then we cannot intelligibly conceive of the same emotion expressed in different media. This dance, under a particular interpretation, is the criterion of a particular feeling which can be identified in no other way. If the object is changed, to poetry for example, then the criterion is changed, and with it the emotion. This is not to say that there is no relation at all between different art forms. As we have seen, art grows out of, and in turn contributes to, the life of people in a community. Art emotions could not be understood without an understanding of life emotions, hence different art forms from the same socio-historical context may well show certain similarities, in a relatively broad, undifferentiated sense. And understanding one art form may contribute to some extent to understanding another, since each is both a reflection of and an influence on a cultural ethos, in isolation from which art would be incomprehensible.[1] But, ultimately, appreciation of art concerns particular discrimination. To take an obvious example, there is a sense in which it could be said that both Mozart's Fortieth Symphony and Gray's *Elegy* express the same emotion, namely sadness, but an interest in art is not an interest in such broad classifications. The more deeply one becomes immersed in an art form, the more specific become one's responses.

It should be added that a comparable failure of discrimination would be equally odd in the case of life emotions. If

---

[1] I am not denying, of course, the possibility that, say, people with a literary background might be found, generally, to learn painting or music more quickly than those without. This would obviously be a matter for empirical enquiry. It does not affect the logical point which is my present concern.

one person is sad because it is raining, and another sad because of the death of someone close to him, it would be strange, to say the least, to say that each is experiencing the same emotion.

The third objection is more difficult. It is obviously possible, as any teacher knows to her cost, for children to "go through the motions" of dancing while feeling nothing but boredom. We should be clear, though, that this is often recognisable by paying attention to their overt behaviour. It is not necessary to ask a child whether the dance movements are connected up, as it were, to appropriate private feelings, even if we ignore the incoherence of this way of looking at the matter. There may be conflicts of criteria here. A child may say that he is emotionally involved, yet he may be performing in an obviously listless manner. Conversely, it may happen that a child, perhaps because of shyness or fear of derisory remarks from classmates, may perform with evident intensity yet say that he was bored and felt nothing. In such cases we usually take the non-verbal behaviour as the principal criterion. This is, in a conflict between a perceptive, experienced teacher's judgment of the child in action, and what the child says afterwards, we are more likely to take the action as definitive. (It should be remembered that we also discover "crocodile tears" and other forms of deception and self-deception by behavioural criteria. As we saw, in section A, what a person himself says about his feelings is by no means necessarily definitive).

Compare the analogous case of the musician who is stigmatised as a "good technician." This criticism of his performance is not based on an inference to his private emotions. Nor is one likely to change this opinion if he insists afterwards that he was intensely involved emotionally while playing (though this might induce one to pay more careful attention to his playing in future). One's judgment that his rendering lacks feeling is based, precisely, on the way he plays the piece—it is that sort of performance. The difference between playing which is merely technically competent, and that which is not only technically competent but also expressive, is not the addition, in the latter case, of an inner feeling in the performer. The difference is to be found in features of the performance itself, which can be discerned by the trained and sensitive listener who is aware of the significance of, for example, subtleties of phrasing and tonal shading.

In learning to dance, children are acquiring skill in manipulating the tools of the medium. Hence, for more sophisticated, adult spectators it may appear exaggerated to suggest that there is anything emotionally expressive in what is going on. Perhaps, indeed, there may not be. It may seem equally risible to talk of expression in relation to the fumbling fingers of the five-year-old on the keyboard. Nevertheless, without a medium there is no possibility of expression, and therefore no emotion either.

We should recognise the significance of the fact that a work of art is both a natural expression and conventional one. This way of putting it will seem a paradox only to those with the common tendency to regard these terms as necessarily opposed to each other. For example, a natural way of expressing some feelings is in words, yet language, the medium of expression, is developed as a matter of convention. Indeed, the acquisition of a certain degree of linguistic facility is a necessary precondition even of the possibility of experiencing some emotions. Fear of continued economic inflation, for instance, could be felt only by someone with a mastery of language. The same considerations apply to dance. Learning to understand dance is to develop an increasing awareness and experience of emotions which can be felt and expressed only in this specific medium.[1] If a dance lacks expressive qualities this is revealed in the performance itself, just as a "technical" piano performance betrays in the playing a lack of feeling.

There is a constant danger, in considering these issues, of sliding into one of two prevalent errors, or of oscillating

[1] The relation of technique to feeling will be further considered in section J (1).

confusedly between them. In a sense of the argument is trying to steer a course between the Scylla of subjectivity and the Charybdis of reductionism or formalism. To say that the movement quality indicates or betrays the emotion may be misleading in its suggestion that the emotion can somehow be identified apart from the movement. That course leads us straight into the perils of the traditional view. Yet we have to be careful about saying that the emotion is a nothing without the physical movement of the dance, because this may seem to suggest that the feeling can be reduced to a purely physical phenomenon. And that course leads us to the perils of behaviourism or formalism. It is as misleading to say that the movement indicates, or is a sign of, the feeling as it is to say that the movement just *is* the feeling. It is false to suggest that the feeling is some *thing* over and above the movement. To keep our heads clear, we need to remind ourselves that to ascribe a particular emotional quality of expressiveness to a dance is to interpret it.

It is, of course, possible for there to be the physical movement without the feeling, as there can be crying without sadness. But just as crying is still a criterion of sadness even though it is possible to have crying without sadness, so a particular movement is characteristic of, is the behavioural criterion for, a particular feeling, even though it is possible to perform the movement without having the feeling.

Perhaps someone would be disposed to object, "In that case how can you *prove* that the dancer is feeling anything as she dances; How can one know for certain?" One wants to ask the objector what he would *count* as proof, or knowing for certain, in this sphere. With what is he comparing it? For the objection betrays a failure to grasp the point of the argument, in that it implicitly appeals to an inappropriate standard of proof or certainty—most likely to a standard drawn from mathematics or experimental science, even though such standards cannot coherently be applied in this quite different sphere. Mathematical or scientific procedures cannot prove that someone who is sobbing is sad. So the complaint that there can be no proof, like the accusation, with which it is often coupled, the aesthetic judgments are purely subjective which we examined in section F (1), reveals a confusion with another type of logical enquiry, with different *kinds* of proof and certainty. And this is as misguided, if less obviously so, as trying to measure with scales the weight of heavy sarcasm.

It should be remembered, too, that in ascribing certain emotions to a movement we take not just the physical movements into account but also the environment. That they are normally performed in a dance studio or on a stage is by no means irrelevant.

H:

DANCE AND EMOTIONAL DEVELOPMENT

(3) Expressive meaning

It is important, here, to distinguish between the meaning of an expressive form and what that form might be used to express. Before going on to explain this, one might point out that to appreciate the significance of this distinction will allow us to understand the value of approaching the problem of explaining expressive meaning through the notion of what the particular dancer or choreographer feels. There are two principal reasons for this. First, the logical difficulty is the same if artistic meaning is regarded as a separate entity from the physical form, whether the meaning is taken to be the feeling of the particular artist, or a symbol of that feeling as it applies to humanity in general, but one can see the character of the problem more clearly in the former case. Second, though the idea that artistic meaning is what a particular artist feels may be mistaken, it does at least contain an important element of truth, which tends to be overlooked, with disastrously misleading consequences, by those who take expressive movement to be symbolic of feeling in general. We shall consider an example of this in section J (2).

We found in section B (3), that the uses of verbal expressions determine their meanings. But there is a distinction to be drawn between the meaning of a word and what the word might be used to mean on a particular occasion. Thus, if I know that your French is inadequate, and that you think "chaud" means "cold", then, in an emergency in France, when I want you to turn on a cold tap, I might well shout "chaud", meaning you to understand it as "cold." Nevertheless, "chaud" does not mean "cold". Yet, though there is a difference between the standard meaning of a word, and what one might use the word to mean on a particular occasion, this does not imply that standard meanings are independent of human uses of language. The point is that it is what the language-using community usually means by its use of an expression which is normative for its meaning. The meaning having been set in this way, though not rigidly or timelessly set, it is possible for individuals to use the word with a different meaning or with no meaning. Yet we should be clear that meaning is still ultimately determined by human usage.

Similar considerations apply to meaning in the arts. A parrot can be taught to recite a Shakespearian sonnet, which would still be expressive, even though the parrot cannot be feeling the emotion expressed in it, since that would require a mastery of language. Similarly, it is conceivable that, in time, a robot may be developed which could be programmed to dance. The dances could still be emotionally expressive even though the robot is incapable of feeling. Both these cases depend upon the logically prior cases of human poets and dancers who do express through the media of poetry and movement respectively what they are feeling. The performances of the parrot and the robot can be understood as expressive only as extensions of the concept of human expression. These examples show that the meaning of an expressive movement may not be what the dancer is feeling at the time, though its meaning is not independent of what people feel, have felt, might feel, when they make use of such a movement. This is a further consequence of the fact that art, like language, is an intentional activity. Both aesthetic meaning and linguistic meaning are ultimately determined by human intentions.

Exclusive concentration either on the work of art itself or on the feelings of the artist, even if this were possible, would be meaningless. It might be illuminating to compare the meaning of a work of art with the attribution of emotional expression to inanimate objects, like the moon or a gnarled tree trunk. Such objects are often said to look mournful or angry and, in a sense, we then tend to respond to them as we would to a human being. Similarly, one could imagine cracks in a brick wall forming a word, which is meaningful even though the wall cannot mean anything by it. The cracks might take the form of a face with a cheerful expression, though a wall cannot be cheerful. The branches of a tree in a high wind might move expressively, though the tree cannot express anything. In each case we have to draw from a context beyond the object itself in order to understand what is attributed to it. And this is how it is that a dancer can perform expressive movement without necessarily feeling what is being expressed. We interpret the movement, we see it in a particular way, and how we see it depends upon complex associations and connections with a whole cultural background. Its meaning is derived from a far wider context than simply the particular feelings of the particular dancer who is performing it, or of the spectators who are watching it.

Yet, though there can be expressive movement without the emotion, there could not be the emotion without the possibility of expressing it in movement. One can compose poetry "in one's head", but not without words. One can do mental arithmetic, but not without a system of arithmetical symbols. One can compose a dance without actually moving, but not without imagining movement. The emotion, to be intelligible at all, must be in *some* form of expression. According to the traditional view, expressive meaning and the medium in which it is expressed are separate, so that the difference between a physical movement, and the same physical movement which now has expressive meaning, is the addition, in the latter case, of a meaning component. The meaning is taken to be a separate, supervenient *thing*, in which case it would make sense to ask the dancer to omit the physical movement, even in imagination, and retain just the expressive meaning.

To repeat the point, the physical movements of dance are the only way in which these emotions can be expressed and experienced, and the only way in which they can be identified. To try to express such a feeling in any other medium of art is to try to express a something which is no longer identifiable, and therefore a nothing.

These considerations allow us to understand more fully what it means to say that the emotion is criterially related to the movement which expresses it, or, if you like, that the emotion is in the movement itself. For this is not to say either that the mover must be feeling the emotion, or that the emotion is nothing but the physical movement. To put it crudely, some movements are sad, for example, even though the dancer may not be feeling sad. Understanding them under that interpretation is to see, respond to, perform them, as sad movements, So to perform and to watch them with involvement and understanding is to experience the emotion. And it is the *only* way to do so. The same applies to the other arts. If art expresses emotions, then each art form has a unique part to play in the development of the emotions. If we want the children and students in our institutions of education to experience a rich and diverse emotional life, we should, *inter alia,* offer to them opportunities in a wide range of the arts.

One further point. Different art forms may be more appropriate for the self-expression, the emotional development, of different personalities. So the more varied the experience of art, within limits, the better the opportunity for finding the most suitable medium for each individual. The limits are imposed by the need to attain a certain degree of competence with the material of each art form, in order to be able to asses its suitability.

Now it might be objected that all this is true but trivial, since it may be equally true that we have highly specific feelings, obtainable and identifiable in no other way, when engaged in a great range of other activities. There may be feelings which are specific to climbing, skiing, swimming, or even drinking three glasses of vintage wine. What is required now, the objection would run, is to show that the feelings which are specific to dance are particularly *valuable* feelings, so that we may be justified in fostering them in our educational system.

The question of value is another question, and is not our present concern, which is to show that if art contributes to emotional development, then each art form has a distinct contribution to make. In any case, questions of value cannot be settled by philosophical considerations alone. A philosophical examination may be able to explain the way in which value judgments can be supported by reasons but it is not philosophy which decides whether a particular reason, or set of reasons, will or should lead us to particular attributions of value.

J:

CONCLUSION

(1) Learning to feel emotions

In section H (2) it was argued that the ability to manipulate the media of particular arts offers the only possibility of expressing certain feelings. Without acquiring a grasp of the form of expression, one would be incapable of the feelings it is used to express. Yet it may still sound odd to speak of learning how to feel certain emotions, for it is easy to overlook the fact that there is a vast range of feelings available only to those who have achieved a level of competence. This is related to Wittgenstein's point (1953, p.208) that it requires an educated imagination to see a triangle as a fallen object:

> In the triangle I can see now *this* as apex, *that* as base—now *this* as apex, *that* as base.—Clearly the words "Now I am seeing *this* as the apex" cannot so far mean anything to a learner who has only just met the concepts of apex, base, and so on.—But I do not mean this as an empirical proposition. "Now he's seeing it like *this*," "now like *that*" would only be said of someone *capable* of making certain applications of the figure quite freely.
> The substratum of this experience is the mastery of a technique.

This notion of the mastery of a technique raises an aspect of interpretative reasoning on which we have so far only touched, but which has important implications for the arts in education, and which, incidentally, creates further difficulties for any theory which tries to equate aesthetic meaning with sensations. For it can be shown that there is a close connection between the imagination and conceptual abilities.

It was a problem for empiricist philosophers, who tended to concentrate exclusively on "pure" sense-impressions, to account for knowledge. A sense-impression cannot, unaided, tell me that an object is a table. All I could know from a sense-impression, in such a case, would be that I am having an impression as of a brown patch. To know that I am seeing a table I have to subsume the impression under a concept. Indeed, I cannot even know that I am having an impression of a brown patch without assuming concepts of colour and shape. The suggestion of a "pure", unconceptualised sense-impression is unintelligible. On the other hand, some rationalist philosophers tended to go to the opposite extreme, and to concentrate upon "pure" thought or concepts as the fount of knowledge. But "pure" concepts, divorced from the deliverances of the senses, are as incoherent as sense-impressions which are brought under no concepts. It is impossible to think of something which is not answerable in some way or other to sensory experiences. This was precisely the point Kant was making in the quotation given in section F (1),—that neither sense-impressions nor concepts, alone, are sufficient for knowledge. To examine these issues would take us into deep philosophical water, but even this brief mention serves to remind us just how fundamental is the type of reasoning which I broadly termed "interpretative." Furthermore, it leads to the point I am now after, which is the interdependence of imaginative and conceptual abilities.

Interpretation involves seeing, recognising or supplying the instantiation of criteria, which presupposes a competent grasp of the respective concepts. To take a banal example, while gazing at a wallpaper with a flowered pattern one might see a certain configuration of lines and colours as a dragon.

To do so presupposes the ability to recognise something as a dragon—to see in the wallpaper pattern the line, colour and movement, which are the instantiation of the criteria for the concept. So to see a triangle as a fallen object, to see a dragon in the wallpaper pattern, requires a certain degree of intellectual organisation of sense-impressions, involving generalisations, relationships and associations. It is possible to make interpretations only to the extent that one has mastered the relevant concepts. Similarly, to appreciate a work of art requires conceptual ability, and the more complex the interpretation required, the greater the intellectual demand. Moreover, it is only at this level of conceptual competence that emotional responses of a corresponding degree of complexity and particularity can be felt.

In section F (4) the point was made that no sharp separation of fact and interpretation is possible when a work of art is considered from an aesthetic point of view. It may be possible to refer to "that picture", or "that frame and canvas and whatever is on it" if one wishes to give a value-neutral, factual, uninterpreted (in one sense) description, but to look at a picture in such a way is not to look at it from an aesthetic point of view. To consider it aesthetically is to interpret it, since there are no value-neutral, descriptive features which are relevant to aesthetic appraisal. It can be appreciated only from a certain point of view, and only to the extent that the relevant concepts have been grasped.

Some emotions, as we found in section H (2), can be experienced only by those with linguistic facility, and they can be as vividly felt as, say, fear of snakes, which might seem an obvious candidate for a "natural", i.e. unlearned, emotional reaction. Fear of bankruptcy and social disgrace, for instance, can be vivid enough to lead to suicide. Yet it would be impossible to feel such a fear without a grasp of the complex ramifications of an economic system, and without having learned to master a language which incorporates the moral values and conventions of a society.

Wittgenstein says, of the mastery of a technique:

But how queer for this to be the logical condition of someone's having such-and-such an *experience*! After all, you don't say that one only "has toothache" if one is capable of doing such-and-such.

Nevertheless, there are many feelings which can be experienced only by those with certain abilities. Any feeling involving the distant past, for example remorse, or involving the future, for example fear of, or hope for, what may happen in six months' time, is limited to a language-user. It would make no sense to suggest that a dog could experience such feelings since he cannot intelligibly be supposed to have mastered the concepts which alone make them possible. (See Jonathan Bennett, 1964, for a discussion of these issues). Similarly a precondition of experiencing the subtle and finely differentiated feelings which are the province of art, is that one should have acquired the imaginative ability to handle the appropriate concepts. Understanding art is not simply a matter of "natural", unlearned feeling as is so often thought by those who accept without question the supposed antithesis between emotion and reason. Whole areas of feeling will remain unknown to those who have not learned to appreciate the arts.

This has important consequences for the arts in education. The more one comes to understand the art form, the more one develops the capacity for fine discriminations of interpretation, and therefore for finely discriminated emotional feelings. Like the grasp of other concepts, it is a matter of degree—the degree of mastery of ability to operate with the relevant criteria. And, as we saw in section F (4), these criteria are derived from the social and cultural life of the community in which the artist is working. In this, too, the arts are analogous to language. It is profoundly mistaken to think of verbal language as a supervenient activity, for it is continuous with non-verbal forms of behaviour. A society without language would be an impoverished society, intellectually and emotionally. Similarly, appreciation of the arts is a matter of both conceptual and emotional abilities which can confer added dimensions to life-situations in the society which gives the arts their meaning. (For a discussion of the way in which the arts can contribute to a deeper appreciation of moral questions, see R.W. Beardsmore 1971). The story is told that a visitor, on hearing that Picasso had completed a painting in half an hour, expressed surprise that it had taken so short a time. Picasso's reply was that it had taken sixty-four years. He was referring, of course, to far more than the attainment of draughtsmanship.

These considerations suggest that there may be some danger in the modern trend towards eclecticism in the arts, if this is taken too far. However interesting and broadening it may be to try to understand the art forms of widely different cultures, such an enterprise might also incur the inability to appreciate *any* art in depth, for at least two related reasons:

(1) Art which is part of one's own social and cultural background allows for greater depth and complexity of feeling, comprehension and creative potential. This includes art which consciously attempts to reject its cultural heritage, since, paradoxically, it too can be fully understood only in relation to what it is trying to reject. Renford Bambrough (1973) makes the general point:

> You cannot seek knowledge unless you already have some knowledge, any more than you can set out to go somewhere without already being somewhere. . . Both in theory and in practice we can start only where we are, and that means that we can never start from scratch. . . The aspiration to make *all* things new is incoherent . . .

(2) Since aesthetic appreciation requires the mastering of a technique, it is unlikely that a level of competence can be attained sufficient to allow for a profound and sensitive feeling for nuances of artistic meaning if one tries to understand too many art forms over too diverse a range of cultures. Similarly it would be difficult to achieve such command of a variety of languages that one could express and understand in each the subtleties of meaning of which

each is capable. It is a common experience that people whose ways of thinking are set by their native language may live for many years in a foreign country without ever achieving a sufficient mastery to appreciate the linguistic subtleties of their adopted country, and therefore the subtleties of feeling expressible in its language.

This suggested warning should not be misconstrued. It is no more a prescription for conservatism in the arts than the analogy with language is a proscription against learning foreign languages. One may gain enlightenment even from a relatively superficial acquaintance with the arts of a very different cultural tradition, partly because art is to some extent an expression of unconscious feelings, some of which may be universally comprehensible in some degree. Nevertheless, though it may be interesting and enriching, beyond a certain point eclecticism may carry with it the penalty of failure to achieve any real depth of aesthetic understanding, and consequently a limited capacity for those shades of feeling the full range of which can be acquired only by someone with a comprehensive grasp of an art form. To determine the point at which the loss may outweigh the gain will be a delicate and pragmatic matter.

J:

CONCLUSION

(2) Intuition

The foregoing discussion leads us to an important topic about which nothing has so far been said directly—namely intuitionism. This omission has now to be rectified, partly because it is so commonly believed that artistic meaning ultimately depends on intuitive knowledge, and partly because any such theory is incompatible with the argument of this book. It will be seen that the notion of the mastery of a technique, which we have just discussed, overcomes the problems which, it is frequently thought, only intuitive perception can overcome. But intuition suffers from deficiencies similar to those of traditional dualism, as we can see by comparing it with telepathy. Take a hypothetical case where John claims to be telepathically sensitive to Henry's thoughts, and it is found that whenever John says he knows what Henry is thinking, Henry confirms it. To subject the claim to more searching examination, Henry is sent to a room hundreds of miles away, with no telephone or other normal method of communication available, and under close observation. To avoid the possibility of collusion Henry is asked, quite unpremeditatedly at 9.00 p.m. to think of a one-eyed, pink-striped hippopotamus. Other observers watch John who, at 9.00 p.m. precisely says "Henry is thinking of a one-eyed, pink-striped hippopotamus." This is impressive, but not yet conclusive, since it may have been a remarkable coincidence. So numerous similar tests are carried out, in different places and conditions, and each time John tells us correctly what Henry is thinking. We have to conclude that the claim to telepathic knowledge is substantiated, and henceforth we shall be justified in accepting what John says about Henry's thoughts without confirmation.

This might seem to show that knowledge derived solely from telepathy is possible, but it is important to see what is the *criterion* of truth in such a case. For, though what John says about Henry's thinking is now accepted as true without further validation, the criterion is conformity to empirically checkable facts, since any claim to telepathic knowledge remains answerable to such facts in the last resort. To bring this out clearly, consider what would be done if we began to doubt John's ability—if, for instance, we suspected that he was losing his telepathic power. Such doubt would be meaningless without some independent and ultimate method of checking his claims. The doubt can be understood only in relation to an underlying ground or standard of truth which is provided by empirical corroboration.

The same is true of intuitive knowledge. Intuition could come to· be accepted as accurate and reliable but only in relation to publicly observable criteria. Intuition cannot by itself be the ultimate ground of knowledge. So while one does not wish to deny the possibility of intuitive knowledge, it is important to be clear that it cannot be the ultimate court of appeal. The fortune-teller's predictive success depends upon correspondence with what is observed to happen.

Intuitionists usually insist or imply that aesthetic meaning is objective, but this is a strange position, for, on their hypothesis, if you and I are looking at the same dance performance, and you intuit one meaning while I intuit another, we are, in effect, in an extreme subjective position. It is impossible to give reasons for our respective interpretations since this would be to appeal to agreed facts or premises lying outside the realm of pure intuitions. We are left so powerless that it cannot even be said that we genuinely disagree, since there is not even a basis for disagreement. If you say "I feel hot" and I say "I feel cold", there is no disagreement between us. And this, at best, is the position to which recourse to intuition must reduce differences of interpretation in the arts, which is a travesty of what actually happens in such cases, for though there are irreconcilable differences of opinion, it is also possible to learn and to change one's views as a result of listening constructively to reasons given for different interpretations and approaches. Even where one's original opinion remains unaltered, to recognise alternative ways of seeing a work of art can be an enlightening experience. For these are differences of opinion, properly so-called, which can engender the rational and illuminating discourse, the exchange of view on interpretation, which is one of the great rewards of involvement with the arts. Each of us is not immutably confined to his own intuition, which cannot be shared or explained.

In fact intuitionism is in a worse case even than this, for it degenerates into the incoherence of the inaccessibly private feelings of the traditional theory, with which it has significant affinities. If aesthetic meaning depends upon intuition, then it becomes undiscussably subjective, and that is to say that no sense can be given to the notion of meaning in this sphere. As in the case of the traditional view, absolutely any meaning could be intuited for any work of art. There could be no correct meaning, since there would be no criterion of correctness—there would be no difference between what seemed to be, and what was, even a broadly correct interpretation. To repeat the point, this is not to deny the possibility of intuitive understanding. It is to insist that such understanding makes sense only against the underlying support of criteria of aesthetic meaning which are constituted by observable features of works of art.

Consequently it is difficult to understand any theory of

meaning in the arts which rests upon intuition, and at least equally difficult to see how it could be proposed in support of the importance of the arts in education. Arnaud Reid (1969), for example, as we noted in section F (2), suggests that it is the influence of traditional expressionist theories of art which has been so largely responsible for the present subordinate status of the arts in educational institutions. In this he is probably right, yet, paradoxically, his own theory's dependence upon intuitive knowledge would, contrary to his intentions, simply help to justify that disparaging view. To be educational an activity has to be rational in some sense. It has to be answerable to objective, publicly observable criteria which can be cited or recognised as reasons. To make the creation and appreciation of the arts answerable to intuition is to reduce them to non-rational activities, which, therefore, cannot be learned and taught. Intuition is proposed in order to bridge the gap between physical manifestation and aesthetic meaning, but it is a bridge which cannot lead anywhere, since each person's intuition is inaccessibly private. And that is to say that we could not intelligibly speak of meaning, evaluation or interpretation in the arts. But when one reads a critical review it is possible to *learn* by appreciating the strength of the reasons given for a particular interpretation by a knowledgeable and perceptive observer. His reasons draw attention to aspects of the work which one had overlooked or construed in another way. To read the work of a Berenson or a Leavis is not merely to be given an account of the writer's intuitions, even if one could make sense of such a hypothesis,—it is to be led to see previously imperceptible shades, tones, nuances, which throw new light on the work under review, and which progressively broaden, deepen and refine one's capacity for appreciation. If someone fails to understand a piece of music, one is not helpless in the face of a faulty intuition. One might play, whistle or sing it to him, stressing certain phrases etc., for, as we saw in section F (2), reasons in the arts are not exclusively verbal, but they are answerable to what is in principle perceptible. And it is precisely this reason-giving characteristic which justifies the claim that the arts can properly be included in the curriculum, for it follows that artistic appreciation and performance can be developed as a result of a fully rational interchange.

Resort to intuition is a natural, almost inevitable result of failure adequately to diagnose some of the deeply ingrained philosophical misconceptions which we examined earlier. Roughly, this occurs in the following ways:

(1) A mistaken view of the emotions creates the problem of getting the feeling into the object, the emotion into the expressive movement, the mental into the physical. This stems from the category error of taking the body and mind to be separate *things*. To hold such a view, even implicitly, as most people do, is to make the emotion inaccessible to external observation. Since the normal perceptual senses are thereby rendered impotent, it is natural to suppose an abnormal, intuitive sense to do the job of reaching the expressive meaning.

(2) An oversimple, restrictive assumption, implicit or explicit, that genuine reasoning must be either deductive or inductive, leads to a denial that the arts can be rational since neither of these paradigms of reasoning is relevant to aesthetics. It is then tempting to assume that artistic meaning must be discoverable by intuition.

(3) The intuitionist recognises that aesthetic meaning is unique, that it cannot be comprehensively conveyed in any form other than this particular expression, that there can be no synonyms in art. It is natural to assume from this that, since the meaning of a work of art cannot be explained in terms of anything else, it can be revealed only by the direct act of intuition. To say that a pillar box is red is to attribute to it the property of redness, so it might seem that to characterise a dance as emotionally expressive is, similarly, to attribute to it a property—in this case that of emotional

expressiveness. Thus a contributory factor to the plausibility of intuitionism is a mistaken theory of meaning. A work of art is taken to be meaningful only to the extent that it stands for or symbolises some other property or entity. If this cannot be perceived it is tempting to assume it must be mental or transcendental, and that the only way to come to know about it is through the metaphysical faculty of intuition.

Suzanne Langer, one of the most influential philosophers in the dance world, as well as in the arts generally, illustrates how easy it is, even for someone of her calibre, to be misled by such assumptions. She is much too sophisticated a thinker to suggest that the meaning of a dance is simply its expressing what the dancer happens to be feeling as she performs. What the artist does, she says, is to project the *form* of feeling.

> Art is the creation of forms symbolic of human feeling. (1953)

So, according to Mrs. Langer, the meaning of any work of art lies in its expression of, or analogy with, a logical form of feeling, hence we can know what a dance means only by recognising the logical form it expresses.

There is an immediate difficulty in accounting for what it might mean to speak of the "logical form of feelings", or of feelings which are not particular. It will be clear from section E (2) that no sense can be made of an emotional feeling which is not normally directed onto an object. Or, as Reid (1969) puts it, feeling which is isolated from a specific feeling *of* is a nonentity. But the point I am after now is that, even leaving aside that problem, since art is said to be a projection of something else, this separates the content from the form, in which case how can we know that this dance does express a specifiable, or indeed any, logical form of feeling? For Mrs. Langer there is only one possible answer—intuition.

> How can the import of an art symbol (i.e. a work of art) be known to anyone but its creator?

By. the most elementary intellectual process ... the basic intellectual act of *intuition*. (1953).

The artist, she says:

formulates that elusive aspect of reality that is commonly taken to be amorphous and chaotic, that is, he objectifies the subjective realm... A work of art expresses a conception of life, emotion, inward reality. (1957)

The genesis of the postulation of these metaphysical entities called "forms of feeling", and of our intuitive knowledge of them in works of art, is the notion that the meaning of a work is what it symbolises—in short that meaning is naming.[1] In this Suzanne Langer is similar to Plato who, as we saw in section B (1), also postulates transcendental Forms as a result of pre-supposing the naming theory of meaning. Mrs. Langer recognises that a dance cannot be an expression of the particular feeling of the dancer, but assumes that it must symbolise something—hence she concludes that it must be a form of feeling. And once a separate realm of being has been supposed, it is almost inevitable that intuition will be the only candidate for the means of knowledge.

Now obviously this is an inadequate criticism of a philosopher who has written as extensively and perceptively about the arts as Suzanne Langer. This is not the place for a detailed examination of her work, but I submit that the most fundamental of her difficulties stems from this preconception about meaning, or "import" as she later calls it. This in turn inevitably separates form and content, i.e. the physical medium and what is being expressed in it, with all the attendant logical problems of bringing them together intelligibly. Mrs. Langer, of course, is by no means unaware that

[1] Of course I do not wish to deny that symbols are used *in* art. It is what Suzanne Langer (1957) distinguishes as the art symbol, i.e. the symbol constituted by the work of art as a whole, which seems to me so misleading.

form and content cannot coherently be separated. She says (1957):

> The art symbol, . . . , *is* the expressive form. It is not a symbol in the full familiar sense, for it does not convey something beyond itself. Therefore it cannot strictly be said to have a meaning; what it does have is import. It is a symbol in a special and derivative sense, because it does not fulfil all the functions of a true symbol: it formulates and objectifies experience for direct intellectual perception or intuition, but it does not abstract a concept for discursive thought. Its import is seen in it; not, like the meaning of a genuine symbol, by means of it but separable from the sign.

This passage reveals the difficulty she is in. A work of art has a meaning in that it is symbolic, yet it cannot have meaning, it cannot be symbolic, because that would imply that the meaning is separate from and somehow projected into the work. The tension is created by a conviction on the one hand that art has expressive meaning, yet a recognition, on the other hand, that it cannot have meaning since that would imply a division of form and content. Recognising, too, that the meaning of a work cannot simply be what the artist is feeling, Mrs. Langer postulates the forms of feeling as providing the meaning element.

But no appeal to a relationship with such a form will make any difference to our saying that *Adagio for a Dead Soldier* is sad. The meaning of this dance has nothing to do, even if it made sense, with the expression of a logical form or feeling. The meaning of the dance is to be seen there, in the dance itself, in the way we interpret it, in the significance and associations of the movements with life situations, and relations with the other arts. Suzanne Langer makes meaning an extra entity, and since it cannot be perceived she has to make it transcendental and discoverable by intuition. Though she insists that the relation between this meaning-entity and the work is very close, it still is not logical, and cannot be, because of her preconception about meaning. And intuitive perception has to be brought in to do the job of recognising this metaphysical entity which is the meaning of import of a work:

> The act of intuition whereby we recognise the idea of "felt life" embodied in a good work of art is the same sort of insight that makes language more than a stream of little squeaks or an arabesque of serried inkspots. (1957).

There is a point here which we shall discuss in the next section, but it has already been stressed that the meaning of anything, art, a word, a chess move, depends upon a convention. We know that this is a sad dance not by intuition, but because of the sort of movements which are used in it. We interpret the dance, and we can give reasons for our interpretation which point out features of the physical movements themselves. Meaning demands a context, it does not depend on something else, lying behind it. Roughly, the meaning of a particular movement is given by the whole dance, the meaning of the dance is given by the dance-tradition of which is a part or extension, and the meaning of that tradition is given by the culture, society, form of life to which it belongs. If human beings were very different and, for example, made quick, light, vivacious movements, with smiling faces, when they were thoroughly miserable, then expressive movements in dance would have to be very different too.

Certainly the dancer and spectator do not have to be experiencing the emotion expressed in a dance. Through the medium of the arts one can explore, and deepen one's insight into the character of an emotion, without necessarily feeling it, but this would be impossible if what was expressed were *totally* independent of human feeling. Hence, again, the advantage of approaching the problem of what is expressed in movement through the notion of what the dancer feels. It is by no means altogether mistaken. It at least keeps artistic meaning firmly involved with the way in which human beings live their lives, rather than projecting it into a metaphysical realm.

Though Arnaud Reid (1969) is aware of these weaknesses

in Suzanne Langer's argument, his dependence upon intuition suggests that, in fact, he continues to share some of her most important presuppositions. He concedes the defects of his earlier "two-term" theory, but it seems to me that he has not yet entirely eradicated it. He says:

> Indivisibility of "content" and "medium" is known in our confrontation with an embodied person to "see" character in a person's face, in his posture and gesture, is neither to perceive his body only nor to apprehend his character through his body, but to apprehend one single embodied person with distinguishable aspects. If I apprehend someone as sad, or wistful, or angry, I am not aware just of ideas, or feelings or a body behaving, but of a person—sad, wistful, angry.
>
> To feel happy, or angry, at ease or in anxiety, is neither mental only nor physical only, but psycho-physical. The aspects are indivisible and convey the idea of meaningful embodied experience.

It is true that when we see character, or emotion, in a person's face or actions we are not attending just to the purely physical in the behaviourist's sense, but it is of the first importance to recognise that we are not attending to *two* indivisibly united things either. The point is that to see character in a person's face is not to see the mental embodied in the physical, it is to *interpret* his physical expression. To ask how the feeling, or the life-experience, gets into the art-object is, similarly, as we have seen already, to go wrong at the outset, for the very formulation of the question makes the fatal presupposition, of the two entities. Admittedly Reid frequently insists, as does Mrs. Langer, that these entities are "indivisible", but however closely they are tied together, to think in terms of two entities is bound, eventually, to lead to a metaphysical answer to the question. "How do we *know* that the feeling, or meaning, is embodied in this physical artefact?" Reid:

> Embodiment can receive all that expression has to offer it; then the creative transformation occurs, the *fiat* of embodiment.

I want to suggest that even so distinguished and perceptive a writer as Arnaud Reid is led to rely on intuition, and the "fiat of embodiment", as a result of insufficiently recognising the crucial relevance to aesthetics of those other areas of philosophical enquiry to which this book has tried to draw attention. Furthermore, I submit that these changes of terminology—Suzanne Langer's discarding of "meaning" for "import", and Arnaud Reid's rejection of "expression" in favour of "embodiment"—are symptoms of, rather than a cure for, the underlying conceptual malaise which is causing all the trouble.

There are not two entities, however inextricably united. If we take the work of art, or the physical behaviour, as a *criterion* of a certain feeling, the problem, in that formulation, dissolves—it cannot be posed, for we do not have two entities, therefore there is no difficulty about getting them together. In the same way, to refer back to section B (4), we do not have two entities—the table and the shape, with the problem of how the shape got into the table.

All cognition of form is intuitive; all relatedness—distinctness, congruence, correspondence of forms, contrast, and synthesis in a total *Gestalt*—can be known only by direct insight, which is intuition. And not only form, but *formal significance,* or import, is seen intuitively . . . , or not at all; that is the basic symbolic value which probably precedes and prepares verbal meaning. (1953).

Arnaud Reid (1969) has a similar conception:

Scientific knowledge, it can be fairly said, does not *consist* of the true propositions which the scientist knows; scientific knowledge is the scientist's intuitive grasp of scientific systems.

Now I agree that scientific knowledge is not ultimately a matter of true propositions. As we saw in section F (1), there is an important sense in which science, like art, depends upon interpretation—the way in which the situation is seen. But is it true that the basis of our understanding, our grasp of an interpretation, depends on intuition? It is tempting to believe so. Similarly, we have seen how far-reaching may be the reasons given to substantiate one's view of the meaning of a work of art. Such reasoning derives its sense and substance from the common system of reference given with a language and way of life, which is the non-collusively agreed basis by which everything is known. The colour orange can be explained as a mixture of red and yellow, but the primary colours cannot be explained by reference to other colours. So how do we know the meaning of "red"? How is it known that this colour is red? It might be thought that we check its congruence with an image of redness which we carry in our minds. But so far from solving the problem, that merely transfers it—for how do we know that the image is red? We should resist the temptation to say that we know by intuition because, as we saw in section J (2), to resort to intuition as the ultimate arbiter is to deny any possibility of knowledge. No, we know that this colour is red, that the word "red" is "more than an arabesque of serried inkspots," because we have learned how to use the concept.

It might be objected, "But the colour which I see as red

J:

CONCLUSION

(4) Expressive movement and intentional action

In Section H (2) it was stated that art is an intentional activity, that aesthetic meaning is determined by human intentions. This raises a number of issues, many of which have been thoroughly debated in recent years. But there is one aspect of the intentional nature of art which seems to have received insufficient attention, and about which it may be worth suggesting a line of thought. For there are consequences here for the recognition of aesthetic meaning, since the character of any intentional action can be recognised only by considering its *relational* significance. To bring out what is meant by this let us refer to the point made in section F (3) that an intentional action is not the same as a physical movement, since the latter can be described in various ways according to one's point of view and one's beliefs about the person performing it. One cannot specify an action, as opposed to a purely physical movement, without taking into account what the agent intended. The movement of someone's leg can be described as "He kicked me" only by making certain assumptions about his intentions. Different intentions prescribe different actions with respect to precisely the same movement. Wittgenstein (1953, § 268) puts the point this way:

> Why can't my right hand give my left hand money?—My right hand can put it into my left hand. My right hand can write a deed of gift and my left hand a receipt.—But the further practical consequences would not be those of a gift.

It is not a physical, perhaps physiological, difficulty which prevents my right hand from paying a debt to my left. A scientific, medical, examination will not be able to explain why my right hand cannot carry out this action, since I am quite capable of performing the requisite physical movement, and anyway precisely the same movement could pay a debt to someone else. The difficulty is logical. It is logically impossible to pay a debt to oneself whatever movement one performs, because one cannot have the required intention. Yet a physical movement does not become an intentional action by the addition of a mental event called an intention. Intentions are discovered by observing physical behaviour, even though they are not the same as physical behaviour from a scientific point of view, since intentions interpret or describe that behaviour. A narrow concentration upon the mechanical or physical aspects of the movement, or upon the sensation of the mover, is insufficient to tell us what *action* was performed. For that certain intentions have to be ascribed to the mover, and that requires a wider view which will allow us to interpret the movement by relating it to its context. Just as a chess move and a word-meaning are incomprehensible in isolation, so an action description can be given and understood only in relation to a situation. For example, weeping behaviour, taken by itself, may be described in terms of grief, joy, frustration or other emotions, or of pain, or even of the result of peeling onions. Only set in wider behaviour patterns, and particularly, as we found in section E (2), in its direction onto an object, does it become recognisable as a criterion of a specifiable emotion. And this applies equally to understanding the aesthetic meaning of movements in dance. This is not to say that one has always to be conscious of the context, or to examine the surrounding behaviour in order to describe an action, any more than a comprehensive foray into the relevant social history is necessary in order to appreciate Renaissance art, since the background or context is usually implicit.

These aspects of the meaning of actions we have already examined, but the point I am now raising, though connected, is somewhat different. For an interesting problem arises where two dancers successively perform the same solo dance, and the context, in every respect, including the movements themselves, appears to be almost indistinguishable, yet there may nevertheless be a vast difference of aesthetic meaning. One dancer may suffuse the same movements with an entirely transformed expression, just as different actors can transform the significance of the same words, and different conductors the same concerto. The problem is to account for so great a change of expressive meaning arising from almost indiscernible physical changes. It is this sort of situation which tempts some to suppose that the difference can be ascribed only to an inner mental event in the dancer, which must be accessible only to intuitive perception, since the observable difference is barely perceptible by the normal senses.

But we do not need, even if it were intelligible, to turn to intuition for an explanation. It is true, as we saw in section F (3), that even a fine shade of difference between one physical movement and another may considerably affect our interpretation of the interconnected web of movements which comprise the dance. Considered *non*-relationally the physical difference may be insignificant, but its importance from the point of view of aesthetic quality or meaning derives from its internal relation to other movements of the dance, and this may be of profound significance. It may so illuminate our way of seeing other aspects of the performance as to reveal a radically altered interpretation of the whole dance. So though, in isolation, it might appear trifling, in the light it sheds on the complex of movements into which it is woven, in virtue of its relation to them, it may determine a centrally different criterion from our previous conception of and response to the dance. Perhaps it will clarify the point to cite the analogy of an actor playing first the part of an angry man, then the part of a man pretending, convincingly, to be angry. Performed by a competent actor, the differences in gesture, and facial and verbal expression, may be very slight indeed, yet they may give a new perspective which will affect one's view of the whole performance, and indeed of the play itself. Irony, too, can be used again to provide a good illustration of the same point, since the ironist treads a tightrope—the better the irony, the narrower the rope. And the cost of failure is that the work will be taken as support for what it is in fact deriding. Yet the very point and character of subtle irony contributes to the danger of misconception, since fine discrimination is often required to recognise the meaning as ironical, rather than taking it at face value. Here, too, the situation in art is continuous with that in the emotions outside art, for sometimes only a slight difference of physical behaviour allows one to distinguish between anger and fear. Though physically slight, it can bring a whole complex of actions under a new description, imbuing each with a changed significance. The pattern of someone's behaviour is now seen in a different light as we attribute to him different intentions.

This brings out more clearly the resemblance between what the psychiatrist often tries to do for his patient, and the reasoning which is characteristic of aesthetic interpretation. The psychiatrist tries to bring his patient to recognise for himself that his actions reveal unconscious intentions and emotions of which he was unaware, or which he had misinterpreted. It is hoped that in this way the patient will come to see that there is a relational pattern in his actions which determines a significantly different interpretation of his intentions and thus a different description of those actions. This reinterpretation defines different criteria, and therefore different emotions, from what he had previously assumed.

There may even be a danger of misapprehension in the suggestion that meaning needs a context, if this is taken to imply that the action, or word, stands out against it like a silhouette. In fact the action or word is itself an inter-dependent part of a context from which it derives its meaning and to which it contributes meaning. Neither is intelligible without the other. So that a particular expressive movement depends, for its meaning, upon its relation to other observable features of the dance, while the dance as a whole gives significance to each movement in it. Moreover, by virtue of its relation to other movements, a slight change of emphasis in one movement can transform the significance of the performance as a whole. To repeat the point, the same physical movement may be a completely different action in a different context, and conversely an almost imperceptible alteration in a single movement could change the whole meaning of an otherwise identical performance. To discern and recognise the character of such physically slight, yet artistically significant distinctions, requires sensitivity, insight, understanding. It is an acquired ability, though it is continuous with the ability to make discriminations of criteria in life-situations.

SUMMARY
OF THE ARGUMENT

A

The most commonly accepted theory of how emotions are expressed in movement can be seen to be a species of the traditional, dualist, view of the relation of mind to body. This view depends upon an inference from outer physical actions to inner mental events, but in this sphere there cannot be an inference, since we can never reach the inner events.

B

The plausibility and pervasiveness of the traditional view of the mind can be traced to two fallacious, if very natural, assumptions about meaning in language. These are, first, that the meaning of a word is what it stands for, and second, that we can be said to know the meaning of a word only if we can define it. These mistaken assumptions lead to a misconceived theory of the symbolic meaning of art and expressive movement. ·

C

However, though no sense can be made of an inference from outer behaviour to inner feelings, this does not mean that therefore expressive actions are, in principle, comprehensively explicable in scientific terms. This would overlook explanations in terms of reasons, and it would ignore the feeling itself.

D

It may help to locate the logical character of the problem of the mind/body relation, and therefore of how physical movement can be emotionally expressive, to compare some proposed solutions. When their respective strengths and weaknesses are considered, it becomes clear that a guaranteed connection is required between the physical and the emotional or mental.

E

A logical guarantee is the only possibility, but first we must disabuse ourselves of a common, but too narrow, conception of logic. A criterion is also a logical relation, and it is crucial to our enquiry to be clear about its character, especially with respect to the emotions.

F

The notion of the criterion allows us to understand the important part which reasoning can play in relation to the emotions, including those expressed in dance and the other arts. The tension between the emotional character of art, and the possibility of rational exchanges of view about it, is dissolved when one recognises that such tension is an inevitable result of the underlying traditional theory of the emotions. Reasoning is characteristic of art-appreciation. It consists of arguing for an interpretation, for a way of

conceiving the performance or work, and it depends, ultimately, for its substance, on cultural and social conventions,
on a way of life.

G

It is sometimes suggested that the aesthetic meaning of
dance depends not on the emotions, but on the physical
sensation of moving, which can be communicated to
spectators, or other dancers, by causing in them a feeling of
empathy. But no causal explanation can be adequate to
account for meaning.

H

The consequences of the argument of section F are now
considered from the point of view of how the arts can
contribute to emotional development. A common assumption about transfer from one art form to another is shown to
depend on the traditional view of the emotions. Since the
feelings expressed in dance are inseparable from the physical
movements employed, these feelings can be experienced in
no other art form, though that is not to say that the
performer is necessarily experiencing them.

J

The foregoing discussion implies that feelings can be
learned by mastering certain techniques. This overcomes the
problems which often lead to the appeal to intuitive
knowledge upon which so many theories of aesthetics
depend. Intuition is an almost inevitable metaphysical consequence of the failure to diagnose the pernicious presuppositions about meaning and the emotions which we
examined earlier. But it is neither necessary nor possible to
appeal to intuitive perception to give us the basis of
knowledge, or to account for the great differences of
aesthetic meaning which may be the consequence of minute
differences of physical movement.

BIBLIOGRAPHY

Anscombe, G. E. M. (1966). Pretending. In S. Hampshire (Ed.) *Philosophy of Mind.* New York: Harper & Row.

Atkinson, R. F. (1969). *Conduct: an introduction to moral philosophy.* London: Macmillan & Co. Ltd.

Bambrough, J. R. (1963). *The Philosophy of Aristotle.* New York: Mentor.

Bambrough, J. R. (1973). To reason is to generalise. *The Listener* Vol. 89, No. 2285. 11th Jan. p. 43.

Beardsmore, R. W. (1971). *Art and Morality.* Macmillan Press Ltd.

Bennett, J. F. (1964). *Rationality.* London: Routledge & Kegan Paul Ltd.

Bennett, J. F. (1966). *Kant's Analytic.* London: Cambridge University Press.

Best, D. N. (1973). Empirical examination of dance—a reply. *British Journal of Physical Education,* Vol. 4, No. 2.

Bondi, H. (1972). The achievement of Sir Karl Popper. *The Listener.* Vol. 88, No. 2265, August 24th, pp. 226-227.

Casey, J. (1966). *The Language of Criticism.* London: Hutchinson & Co. Ltd.

Charlton, W. (1970). *Aesthetics: an introduction.* London: Hutchinson & Co. Ltd.

Diffey, T. J. (1973). Essentialism and the definition of 'art'. *British*

Journal of Aesthetics, Vol. 13, No. 2.

Elton, W. (1954). *Aesthetics and Language.* Oxford: Blackwell.

Hawkins, A. M. (1964). *Creating Through Dance.* New Jersey: Prentice-Hall Inc.

H'Doubler, M. N. (1957). *Dance. A Creative Art Experience.* U.S.A.: University of Wisconsin Press.

Hepburn, R. W. (1965). Emotions and Emotional Qualities. In C Barrett (Ed.) *Collected Papers on Aesthetics.* Oxford: Blackwell.

Kant, I. (1929). *Critique of Pure Reason.* Translated by N. Kemp Smith. London: Macmillan & Co. Ltd.

Kennick, W. E. (1965). Does Traditional Aesthetics Rest on a Mistake? In C. Barrett (Ed.) *Collected Papers on Aesthetics.* Oxford: Blackwell.

Laban, R. (1971). *Rudolf Laban Speaks about Movement and Dance.* Addlestone, Surrey: Lisa Ullman, Laban Art of Movement Centre.

Langer, S. (1953). *Feeling and Form.* London: Routledge & Kegan Paul Ltd.

Langer, S. (1957). *Problems of Art.* London: Routledge & Kegan Paul Ltd.

Locke, J. (1961). *Essay Concerning Human Understanding.* J. W. Yolton (Ed.), London: Dent.

Meerloo, J. A. M. (1962). *Dance Craze and Sacred Dance.* London: Peter Owen Ltd.

Phillips, D. Z. (1970). *Death and Immortality.* London: Macmillan & Co. Ltd.

Reid, L. A. (1969). *Meaning in the Arts.* London: George Allen and Unwin Ltd.

Rhees, R. (1969). *Without Answers.* London: Routledge & Kegan Paul Ltd.

Ryle, G. (1949). *The Concept of Mind.* London: Hutchinson & Co. Ltd.

St. Denis, R. (1941). *Dance As Spiritual Expression.* Edited by F. R. Rogers. New York: Macmillan & Co. Ltd.

Sartre, J-P. (1969). *Being and Nothingness.* Translated by H. Barnes. New edition. London: Methuen.

Shawn, T. (1946). *Dance we Must.* London Dennis Dobson Ltd.

Shawn, T. (1963). *Every Little Movement.* New York: Dance Horizons Inc.

Shoemaker, S. (1963). *Self-Knowledge and Self-Identity.* Cornell University Press.

Strawson, P. F. (1966). *The Bounds of Sense.* London: Methuen.

Weitz, M. (1962). The Role of Theory in Aesthetics. In J. Margolis

(Ed.) *Philosophy Looks at the Arts*. New York: Charles Scribner's Sons.

Wisdom, J. (1952). *Other Minds*. Oxford: Blackwell.

Wittgenstein, L. (1962). *Tractatus Logico-Philosophicus*. Translated by Pears & McGuinness, London: Routledge & Kegan Paul Ltd.

Wittgenstein, L. (1953). *Philosophical Investigations*. Oxford: Blackwell.

Wittgenstein, L. (1958). *The Blue and Brown Books*. Oxford: Blackwell.

Wittgenstein, L. (1966). *Lectures and Conversations on Aesthetics, Psychology and Religious Belief*. Oxford: Blackwell.

Wittgenstein, L. (1967). *Zettel*. Oxford: Blackwell.

Wollheim, R. (1968). *Art and its Objects*. New York: Harper & Row.